I'm A Grandmother!!
Now What?!

*Great Ideas on How to Have Fun
with Your Grandchildren!*

Toni "Mimi" Stone, a Grandmother

Bloomington, IN

authorHOUSE™

Milton Keynes, UK

AuthorHouse™
1663 Liberty Drive, Suite 200
Bloomington, IN 47403
www.authorhouse.com
Phone: 1-800-839-8640

AuthorHouse™ *UK Ltd.*
500 Avebury Boulevard
Central Milton Keynes, MK9 2BE
www.authorhouse.co.uk
Phone: 08001974150

First published by AuthorHouse 01/09/06

ISBN: 1-4259-0504-8 (sc)

Library of Congress Control Number: 2005910978

*Printed in the United States of America
Bloomington, Indiana*

This book is printed on acid-free paper.

Written in honor of our grandchildren,

Sara Grace, Ashley Elizabeth, Luke David

and

other grandchildren we have not met yet!

Acknowledgements

My sincerest thanks goes to the many grandmother friends who have contributed their creative ideas for this book: Kathy Adams, Bev Babcock, Linda Black, Lois Brewster, Suzanne Carpenter, Dorothy Carter, Diane Coffey, Dona Cooper, Pat Downs, Karen Gallagher, Carol Headrick, Anita Ibison, Nancy Powell Kehn, Marian Ledgerwood, Judy Morrison, Mary Ostlund, Mary Anne Price, Georgan Reitmeier, Sue Timberlake, Betty Tower, and Lou Watkins.

A special thanks to dear friends Carol Headrick and Betty Tower whose stories of wonderful times with their grandchildren *first* made me realize that stories like these needed to be shared. Thanks for their time in proofing the manuscript and for encouraging me to get it published. A big thanks, to Dona Cooper for sharing her wonderful poetry!

My heartfelt thanks go to my *dear* husband, and editor, Bill, a terrific "Papa", who encourages me daily. We are actually a team in this "grandparenting" adventure, and I know we both will benefit from the ideas in this book.

I am indebted, of course, to my own dear Grandma Mellie, who made me want to aspire to be a devoted grandmother like her. I pray that I will be remembered by my grandchildren as I remember her—with great love and affection and deep appreciation for her influence on my life.

Of course, nothing is possible for me without the gifts God has given me. I seek constantly to fulfill His purpose in me and pray that this book is a part of His will for my life.

Contents

Preface   xiii

1   "I'm a Grandmother!"   1

2   Memories of Our Grandmothers   6

3   Play-time With Grandma   16

4   Story Time With Grandma!   31

5   Learning from Grandma   42

6   Holidays with Grandma   52

7   Birthdays with Grandma   71

8   Travels with Grandma   83

9   Finding God With Grandma   97

10   Long Distance Grandmas!   108

11   What Do You Wish You had Done
     with Your Grandchildren??   114

Appendix A: Toys and Games   117

Appendix B: Children's Books   122

Appendix C: Ways to Spoil your Grandchild   136

Appendix D: Grandparents who are Parents   139

I'M A GRANDMOTHER!!
NOW WHAT?!

*Great Ideas on How to Have Fun
with Your Grandchildren!*

Preface

What inspired me to write this book? The answer—great stories of friends who were very creative grandmothers!! I was learning from them and felt that their stories needed to be shared with others!! Many of the things in the book can be done, and often are done with parents, but the truth is, parents are VERY busy!! If both parents are working outside the home, they have very little "play time" with their children. Even when Mom or Mr. Mom stays home with the children, keeping up with the day-to-day chores—cleaning, cooking, washing, etc.—leaves them little "free" time, so grandparents have the privilege of "having more fun" with their grandchildren.

My grandmother mentor and friend, Marian Ledgerwood, reminded me, "A young mother needs help and encouragement, and the grandmother, in turn, is rewarded by helping the young mother and spending quality time with the baby. I spent many hours rocking my grandbaby—singing to him, pushing him down the street in the baby buggy or the stroller, and playing with him. When he was a little older, there were books to be read and household chores to do together while my daughter shopped, or sewed, or caught up on some rest."

Another dear friend, Betty Tower, believes that the secret to successful grand-parenting is doing the same thing over and over—developing traditions. "Nanny Betty" to toddler granddaughters and "Mom" to her older grandsons, she has established many traditions over the years:

1. Celebrating birthdays together
2. Decorating a birthday cake according to the child's interests
3. Having a gingerbread house decorating contest during the Christmas holidays
4. Putting money into accounts for birthdays
5. Going to church together on Christmas Eve

Although my initial purpose in writing this book was to help grandmothers (or grandparents) have fun with their grandchildren—providing ideas for all kinds of activities we can do with them—I believe that the key to being a positive force in the lives of our grandchildren is not in "what we do", but instead in "who we are" when we are with them. I think this is what this book is all about.

The grandmothers I interviewed for this book would all agree with this statement made by one insightful grandmother: "The best advice I can give to any grandparent is to love your grandchildren, no matter what their age. Give them lots of hugs and kisses, and most of all, enjoy them!! They are such a blessing!" Another added, "In interacting with our grandchildren, we always try to be POSITIVE!" Howard Hendrix said to a troubled young person one day, "I've heard a lot about you, and I don't believe any of it!" Grandparents can provide that "second chance"!

"I'M A GRANDMOTHER!"

First Grandchild
by Dona Maddux Cooper

Just a memory ago
The cradle where you sleep
Rocked your father, little one
And in love's locket where I keep
His picture, now finds yours
Superimposed so that my heart
Cannot at this cherished moment
Tell the two of you apart.

Everyone who *is* a grandmother knows the indescribable and absolute joy that being a grandmother brings! Those who aren't grandmothers can only imagine. Even I, in my pre-Grandma days wondered, "What's the big deal?!" What could be more exciting than having your *own* children??

Some of us had to wait a long time to experience what our grandmother friends talked about. In my case 8 years! My friend, Gayle, became so exasperated by the wait that she started a "support group" for non-grandmothers!!

Once I heard the long-awaited news that I would indeed be so blessed, the question then arose, "What do you want to be called?" "Whatever *she wants* to call me!" was my immediate answer. I didn't care and was very happy with the one she chose–"Mimi". Whether chosen by the grandmother or the grandchild, many creative names emerged among our friends:

"Grandmother" Carol, chosen because that was what she called her grandmother, and because it would be more appropriate as the child grew older.

"Gramouse" Dona, because she did a column in the church newspaper called "Tidbits by the Church Mouse".

Other names include Honey, Honna, Gram, Grams, Gramma, Grammar, Grammie, Mam, Maw, Mamoo, Mema, MeeMaw, Mom, Momo, Mimi, Mums, Nan, Nana, Nanny, or any version of the given name of the grandmother–"Suzy", "Dinah", etc. "Grandma" and "Granny", so common in my day, seem to have lost favor. Just as all names have evolved over the years, "Grandma" now has many "handles". Usually, the first grandchild gets to "name" the grandmother, and it sticks with the subsequent grandchildren as well.

Even with all the joyful anticipation, I could never have fully imagined the thrill of being a grandmother until I actually saw the miracle of birth. Seeing this beautiful life emerge, independent of the womb that had nurtured it for nine long months brought tears of joy! One of my friends told a story about a first-time grandmother, who received a video of her newborn grandchild. The camera was focused on the new baby, who did not move for 30 minutes!! *And* she watched every minute of it!! But isn't that the way it is??!! We all just sit around and stare at this little miracle– marveling at its creation!

One of the other unexpected blessings of grandparenthood was being able to watch our own children "parent" their children. I naively thought that they would need lots of advice from us, but what a wonderful surprise to see them doing everything "right"–loving, caring, and attending to every need of this new life. This sometimes meant that they would *ask* for advice, but they were more than capable of this daunting and most important task of parenting! They were doing a great job, and how satisfying it was to watch their "labor of love". That said, what then would be my role as "Grandma"?? To have FUN, of course, and that's what this book is about!

When I asked other grandmothers what they enjoyed most about being "Grandma", I found that their answers would encourage *anyone* to aspire to that role:

"Gramma" Bev Babcock enjoys the genuine shower of affection from her grandchildren whenever she visits. She says, "I know that their parents have taught them to respect their grandparents, but when I go to visit, they seem so genuinely excited and thrilled to see me. They call often to tell me that they miss me, and that is pretty cool!" "Nanny Betty" Tower agrees, "I enjoy

HUGS the most!   No one can tell you how much you will love this little stranger!"

"Grammar" Pat Downs feels it is a God-given privilege to watch her grandchildren grow and develop in their own special ways.   She marvels at all of their unique personalities –"appreciating Jack's kind heart, hearing Zeke's funny stories, loving Mary Kate's little girl giggle and her love of purple, anticipating Trip's playing big-league football, and melting over Tucker's dimpled smile."

She adds, "They are their own little people, yet they show fleeting glimpses of familiar features and gestures that are precious reminders of our own young children. These flashbacks are serendipitous, going unnoticed to others, thus making them unique blessings to us, as grandparents."

"Mema" Lois Brewster thinks the best times are when "I get to cuddle up and read one-on-one with a grandchild. I also love watching them grow and learn to become loving, responsible people." She has made wonderful soft cloth books for each of her grandchildren when they were born, so she could begin reading with them first thing!

"Grandma" Mary Ostlund from Cheyenne, Wyoming, says what she enjoys most is just being with the grandchildren–"whatever we are doing– playing Scrabble, making cookies, watching a movie or listening to music, eating, shopping, being helped with my computer work–their presence is a joy!"

"Nan" Georgan Reitmeier loves to just "LISTEN to them–pretending with toys, tickle time, pouring water on each other in the pool–the simple things." She also loves watching their inquiry and growth in communication. "I love to interact with them and watch their little minds churn." "Gramouse" Dona Cooper enjoys "those sweet notes in the mailbox!"

"Momo" Suzanne Carpenter thinks it's just plain FUN!!! Watching them grow–watching them interact– seeing the differences in personality from the very beginning. Parents are often SOOO serious about the responsibility of parenting. Grandmothers can laugh because we have perspective. "Been there, done that" and have survived!! We are satisfied."

Grandmother "Dinah" (Diane) Coffey says that she enjoys just watching them! "I love to stay at their houses, seeing their lives and what they do–what their interests are."

It's the diversity that intrigues "Nana" (Nancy) Kehn, an Arkansas grandmother of eight. "We have a couple of artists, a dancer, a horseback rider, a computer whiz, a couple of comedians, but next week . . . who knows?! It's interesting, delightful and sometimes challenging!"

Having been a grandmother now for a few years, I would agree with all of these responses, as well as the one from "Grams" Mary Anne Price, grandmother to 16, who says that she enjoys the "blessing of having healthy, happy, and fun grandchildren". "Honna" Judy Morrison and others summarize all of our feelings well, with the enthusiastic answer to the question, "What do you enjoy most about being a grandmother?" She replies, "ABSOLUTELY EVERYTHING!"

Chapter Two

MEMORIES OF
OUR GRANDMOTHERS

It was impossible to think of what we would do as grandmothers without thinking about our own grandmothers–many, but not all, recalling wonderful memories of times passed with them! My most pleasant childhood memories were those associated with my Grandma Mellie Maurer in Greenfield, Oklahoma. My friend, Carol, reminded me that our grandmothers didn't "drop everything" when we came to visit! They had chores to do, so we just "tagged along", watching them–learning from them. They were our first mentors!

I remember Grandma Mellie's wringing the head off a chicken, picking the feathers off, and boiling it in a big pot on her kerosene stove. But there were more pleasant memories as well. I remember "helping" her do chores–getting the mismatched silverware out of the old cupboard, setting the Fiesta ware on the old oak table, and adding the yellow color packet to the oleo. Later she would teach me how to embroider. I have treasured the memory of her spending time with me as well as the skill itself.

I remember the old mantel clock on top of the dining room cupboard chiming as my brother, sister and I lay on the day "bed", which was only a grid of wires drawn over a steel frame with old quilts on top. Grandma would lie down with us while we looked out the window, watching the tiny lights scooting along the highway a half mile away, and listening to us ask our childish questions. I remember her getting up in the middle of the night to take us to the "outhouse", OR if it was just too cold, showing us the way to the "chamber pot" on the back porch.

I remember the ice man's delivering ice for their "ice box" and her "slopping" the pigs. They saved all the "scraps"–nothing was wasted! There was no air-conditioning or fans, so we would lie IN the window to get every breath of air on a hot summer night. I remember her canning 104 quarts of green beans from Grandpa's garden and storing them in the cellar, which served as a refuge from tornadoes, as well. Nearby was the old pump and cistern where we got our water.

I remember the old feather bed, which was ours when the adults didn't come with us, and free-standing closets or "armoires" or simply curtains drawn across a part of the bedroom–or what served as a multi-purpose room. On special occasions these curtains would be opened to reveal an old pump organ that Grandpa would play, accompanied by a "juice harp" in his mouth. He wasn't a "warm, fuzzy" type, BUT this memory of him will endear him to me forever!

I remember walking to "town" along the dusty roads. It was only three blocks away, but I was so excited to make this "journey". There was the telephone office, where Grandma worked magic at the switchboard; the drugstore, with a fountain; a grocery, a tiny post office, and an old Baptist church with a steeple, where Grandma would take us when our visit extended to Sunday.

I remember feeling very secure! At that time my grandparents had been married almost fifty years. There were no unkind words spoken between them. Grandma Mellie had sparkly blue eyes, wore feed-sack dresses with aprons over, had short white hair, cute little smile, and sagging breasts to her waist. My Grandpa Maurer wore overalls and a hat to protect him from the sun when in his garden. He listened to the radio while smoking his pipe, and often was gone to "town" to play dominoes with his friends. Life was very simple, and they seemed to enjoy our visits as much as I did.

In college I would do a paper on "The History of the English Language", which would require an interview with an elderly person to trace how the language had changed over the years. I would choose to interview my Grandma Mellie, of course, and what a wonderful time we had! Sofa–divan; good food–good grub; etc. How thankful I am that we had that time together! To most she would seem quite ordinary–to me she was truly *extra*ordinary!

OTHER POIGNANT MEMORIES...

My friend Dona Cooper has recorded memories of her grandmothers in verse:

GRANDMOTHER WILSON
from Family Ties by Dona Maddux Cooper

Noon dishes done,
  she sits for a spell
    in a ladder back
      cane-bottom chair.
Her small, bare feet
  sun-browned
    from hoeing her garden
      are perched on the second round.
From her hair, pewter in color,
  she takes the pins
    and places them
      in her aproned lap
The ticking of the mantel clock
  matches her rhythm
    as she runs the fine tooth comb
      through time-thinned tresses.
Again
  and
    again
      and again.
When every hair
  has been pulled tightly
    back into place,
      she makes a knot,
And then
  reaches for her Bible.

Both of Dona's grandmothers cooked on wood
stoves. They would rub ears of corn together to get corn
for popping and would pop it in an iron skillet. Her
poem, "Popcorn Tradition" from *Family Ties* records
this memory clearly:

> From the bushel basket
> she took the ears of corn,
> deftly rubbing them together,
> two at a time,
> until the yellow seeds
> Fell into the dark brown bowl
> on her aproned lap.
> The cobs went
> into the kindling box
> beside the big black
> kitchen stove.
> After stoking the fire,
> she added a lump of lard
> to the deep skillet
> and when it sizzled; the grain.
> The popping began, sending forth an aroma
> that permeated the log house
> and escaped
> to the southwest corner
> of the woodshed
> where the little girls had gone
> to fetch Winesaps,
> buried in the apple hole.

That same aroma greeted her husband
and sons as they opened the door
bearing tin buckets
of warm milk.
The family gathered around
the lamp-centered pine table
to eat their Sunday night supper
of popcorn,
while she read aloud
another chapter
from *Huckleberry Finn*.

Both of Dona's grandmothers lived in Missouri, and her family visited them on vacations. She remembers the BIG meals–fried chicken, mashed potatoes and several jellies–homemade, of course! "This was the way they showed their hospitality." Sometimes the men would go squirrel hunting, and they would have fried squirrel for breakfast, with biscuits and squirrel gravy. They had a long table with benches, which was needed to seat their large family. They were farmers–there were few toys, but they had cousins to play with. "These were happy times!"

Dona remembers that Grandmother Wilson cried when they came *and* when they left. She lived to be 92, but would say every time they would leave, "I may not live to see you again." Dona captured this moment in her book, *Pen Points*.

AND IT CAME TO PASS

Every summer
For years and years
We'd go to grandmother's
Where her ready tears
Of happiness would greet us.
And sad ones bid us goodbye.
I'll not live to see you again."
Was always her parting cry.
And I would hug and cling to her
Believing her words were true–
And so they were the summer
That she was 92.

Bev Babcock remembers her Grandmother Garrett as an eternal optimist! She loved to whistle, and her favorite song to whistle was "There's an Old Spinning Wheel in the Parlor". She even continued to whistle when there were five stars on the flag, which was hanging in her front window representing five of her children who were serving in World War II. Bev learned optimism and perseverance from her grandmother and also an appreciation for beauty. She always had flowers blooming in her yard and on her front porch.

Betty Tower lived in the same town with her grandmother and remembers her pretty furniture, *Readers' Digest* magazines, a gumdrop tree and family reunions, which continue to this day! "She would always try to get me to eat oatmeal–which I am finally doing at 60." (We can't underestimate those "seeds planted"!)

Judy Morrison remembers her grandmother's hands crocheting and brushing her long hair. She learned to love flowers from her grandmother.

Mary Anne Price remembers her grandmother's coming to her school to tell stories of her travels.

Anita Ibison's most vivid memory of her grandmother was watching her stand in front of the window at sunrise and praying. I learned from my grandmother that God is real and He cares about me."

Diane Coffey learned an "I can do attitude" from her grandmother, who raised grandchildren–even great grandchildren–into her 80's!. "She was selfless and strong. She would sew for me, in spite of the fact that I never wanted to try on anything."

Georgan Reitmeier remembers sleeping with her grandmother on a feather bed on her screened-in porch. "As we lay down, I could no longer see her, for her weight puffed the feather mattress around her. I would call, 'Where are you Grandma?', and she would answer in her strong, low voice, 'Well, right here, Georgan!' Then I could fall asleep to her soft snore."

She also learned from her grandmother how to be a peacemaker. "My mother and daddy would start to fuss, and Grandma would always point out in her low voice, 'Florence, (her daughter), George is such a good man. Leave him be!'"

Even those who didn't have a very close relationship with their grandmothers relate things they learned from them. Mary Ostlund says that she learned the names of many flowers in her garden and remembers their "fun time" was catching Japanese beetles for which she and her sister were paid a penny each.

She remembers that her grandmother was always well groomed. She wore her long gray hair in a bun, was "well-corseted", and seemed to wear mostly black and white dresses. "I still make an applesauce cake from her recipe–and smile when I read the words 'beat vigorously'." She died at age 96 and had the most beautiful skin! She always told me to "wash well and thoroughly" (her words) and to "cream, cream, cream". If you could see Mary's beautiful skin, you would know that she learned that lesson well!

Lois Brewster, who is now in her 80's, remembers her grandmother as a creative and talented seamstress. "When I was about 5, she threaded a needle for me and began to teach me to sew. I remember she tied a tiny knot next to the needle so the thread would not come out as I applied my initial efforts." Lois now uses this talent in creating soft cloth books for her grandchildren and many other lucky children. She also attributes her appreciation of flowers and birds to visits to her Grandma's house.

Carol Headrick's most precious memory of her grandmother was their exchange of letters. Although Carol saw one grandmother every Sunday, she was closer to Grandmother Ruby, whom she only saw Christmas and Easter, because *she* wrote letters! Later Carol would ask her advice on things, and she was mentored through the words of these letters. She died when Carol was 14, but she made a lasting impression! Carol now writes to her own grandchildren. She gives them stationery and stamps. Some are pre-addressed to her; some to the other grandparents, some to their great-grandmother, Carol's mother. Carol is quick to point out that it's okay to e-mail too. Schedules are so packed–children are so busy!

She remembers holiday traditions –"real trees; a cold house and cuddling under a fluffy comforter, listening to adults talk after she went to bed". She remembers exploring the attic and playing dress up. She remembers her grandmother's feeding, killing, cleaning, cooking, and eating chicken! She remembers, too, that they had no debt!

Carol learned many lessons from her grandmother, the most important, perhaps was to continue learning. She was diabetic, and knowing that someday she might be blind, she taught herself to type, so she could continue to communicate. She gave herself insulin shots and would put her feet in ice water, then hot–to increase circulation.

What are your memories of your grandmothers?? What will our grandchildren remember about us?? We hope, of course, that they will have fond memories of our times together. In the next chapter I will share ideas from some very creative grandmothers. I hope you can use these ideas to make wonderful memories with your grandchildren!

Chapter Three

PLAY-TIME WITH GRANDMA

"What do we do all day??!!"

What we do with our grandchildren has a "trickle down" effect. If we provide "memorable times", they will mimic what we do with their own children and grandchildren, so our investment of time and creativity will be well spent–will create a legacy that will affect future generations.

When Grandma gets past "staring" at the newborn, and he leaves her cuddling arms to toddle off to discover the world, the modern-day grandmother, with curiosities strewn throughout her house, must find ways to occupy the little one. After several months of "tagging" behind them, watching their every move, we decided perhaps we should have a "plan" or at least have some activities in mind when they come to visit. I thought we would try to be proactive rather than reactive! Listed below are some of our early activities:

1. Reading with them. At a very young age, they will back up into your lap ready to enjoy the story and pictures with you. I find the toddler loves the small

board books (something they can handle), pop-up and other activity books, where they can take part; and any books with animals. (See Appendix A for favorite age-appropriate children's books.)

2. Making play-doh together. Although you can buy Play Doh at any store, making it together adds to the fun! and helps them learn to create things from what you have on hand. A fool-proof and often-used recipe is given below:

PLAY DOUGH

Mix together: 3 cups flour
                       1 ½ cups salt
                       6 tsp. Cream of Tartar

Add: 3 T. vegetable oil
                       3 cups water

Stir and cook until mixture pulls away from the sides of the pan, and until, when squeezed, it doesn't stick to your fingers. Add food coloring (and mint flavor, if desired).

Turn out and knead like dough. It will cool off quickly, so the children can knead it, too. Store in a plastic container or baggies.

NOTE: Half of this recipe makes a generous amount.

Use utensils and cookie cutters you have around the house to cut and make shapes. At Christmas time cut out stars, bells, Santas and other holiday shapes. Bake (putting a hole in the top of each for the hanger), then paint and give as gifts to parents and others; OR decorate a small kitchen tree with the grandchildren's handiwork. This activity is fun for any holiday!

3. Make a primitive easel (large rectangular board with "lip" or tray for paints to sit on)—hang it on the back fence and paint on a pretty day. The child can watch or help you build the easel—then you can enjoy painting together.

4. Make low "balance beam" with 1x 6's supported by cinder blocks. Hold their hands until they gain confidence. It provides good exercise and is great for gross motor skills. Perhaps you will have a little Mary Lou Retton or Bart Conners some day!

5. Take a trip to the nearest park or school playground. We have found that this is a "favorite" activity with our grandchildren. Take a picnic to make it a perfect day!

6. Go on a field trip! I'm still learning, and what could be more fun than learning with your grandchildren?! Where could you go?
   Museums—many museums have children's exhibits; some towns have museums just for children; museum of natural history—home to dinosaur bones—is especially popular!

Pet Shop–just browse, or bring home a fish or a hamster

City bus trip–conduct your own tour or just enjoy the ride!

Grocery store–let them help you shop for lunch; get a cookie at the bakery.

Local airport–arrange for a tour, or just watch a plane take off or land

Animal clinic–talk with the vet about care for animals

Bakery–watch the large rotating ovens, giant mixers, etc.

Butcher Shop or Deli–let them cut some meat and cheese for your lunch; go on a picnic

Post Office–write letters or send cards to parents–mail them at the post office

County Fair and Livestock Show–enjoy the 4-H exhibits; look at the animals, etc.

Visit a friend who plays an instrument–have him/her demonstrate

Zoo–always a hit!!

Donut Shop–at Krispy Kreme, you can watch a donut from start to finish!

Nursery–select and bring home plants; let the children help plant them.

Bank–let them watch you make a deposit, or open up an account for them

Farm–let the children see animals, the garden, gather eggs, etc.

Circus–read about it before you go!

Pick wildflowers–put them on the table for everyone to enjoy! or make May baskets and take them to a nursing home.

Pick berries–let them help you make jam

Neighbor's house–one with a new litter of puppies, an aquarium, a bird or a favorite collection–en route, talk about "stop, look, listen" before crossing the street

Library or large bookstore with children's area–for story time, special activities

Garage Sales–give them some change to buy their own treasures. Don't go to too many!

Shopping mall–gets birthday or Christmas presents for Mom and Dad, or just expend some energy!

NOTE: Watch the papers for special "children-friendly" activities in your community! We recently took our grandchildren to a Children's Day at the fairgrounds–lots of fun!!

7. Have tea parties with them!! Pretending at first is just as fun–they don't seem to mind that you are drinking from an empty cup! I wonder sometimes if they just humor us, thinking all the time that we are not in our right minds! One time when our daughter, Stefanie, was about two, she was serving "food" to our guests. One friend, who was kind enough to go along with it, said"Ymmmm! This is so good! What is it?" Stefanie looked at her, a little puzzled, and replied, "Nothing."

It's fun to chat with the grandchildren during these tea parties. Sometimes it is quite revealing, as reflected in another favorite poem from Dona Cooper's *Family Ties*, in which she describes a special tea party with her granddaughter:

TEA FOR TWO

> We had lots of tea parties
> And at one of these,
> I asked my granddaughter,
> "Tell me, please,
> When you grow up
> What will you be?"
> "A teacher," she answered
> Sipping daintily.
> Then she added
> After a second, or two,
> "No, I'll just be
> A plain person like you."

8. Do a variety of puzzles–and don't forget to make your own. Draw a picture together, glue to a stiffer piece of paper, and with their permission, cut it into pieces. Enjoy putting *their* creation back together!

9. Play a variety of games with a simple deck of cards–a great "toy"!! Most all of us have an old deck of cards around–even one without 52 cards will work! They can learn matching by putting all the hearts in a pile, spades in a pile, etc. They can learn to count by counting the clubs or diamonds on a card. They can order from 1 to 10, using Ace to 10. They can play the old "concentration" game, by putting all cards (or ¼ or ½ the deck), face down; then turning them up to find the matching cards. As they get older, there are many traditional card games you can play together.

10. Dominoes–A great tool for some of the same reasons listed for cards. This is even popular with 2-year-olds!

11. Make a "Marble Alley" with a simple shoe box. Take the top off, turn the box upside down. Cut three or four half-circle openings along one side of the open top of the box. Draw numbers above each opening. Roll marbles into the openings. The older children will want to keep score; the younger ones won't care–they'll just enjoy getting the marbles in any of the holes! I put marbles in little paper cups and give one to each child *and* myself.

12. Play "Dress up"!! Every grandmother *must* have a "dress-up" basket!!! You can collect these items from

rummaging through your own closet, if you're a pack rat like me; OR you can shop the garage sales!! Look for old hats, ties, fancy clothes–even old drapes make great robes or trains for queens and kings! You can make a "tu-tu" by sewing lots of layers of inexpensive net onto a ribbon. Put it over a leotard you can pick up at Wal-Mart, and *voila,* you've created a ballerina!! Use your imagination!!   The kids certainly will!!

13. "Hide and Seek" is a favorite with our grandchildren!! Sometimes the oldest, simplest activities are the most fun! No special skills required!

14. Children love to be outdoors! We've enjoyed these activities with our grandchildren:

   - Fly kites
   - "Follow the Leader"–skipping, leaping like frogs, jumping like kangaroos, running like horses, etc. Take turns being the leader.
   - Walk in the yard or neighborhood, looking for signs of spring, fall, etc.
   - Pick vegetables from the garden.
   - Plant some bulbs to come up in spring or summer.
   - Draw with chalk on sidewalks or driveway– trace around their bodies or play Hop Skotch.

15. On a trip to Tulsa to visit our grand-children, we took a scrapbook with photos, post cards, and other souvenirs of a recent trip. They had lots of questions and wanted to look at it over and over again.

Ideas From Other Grandmas

Gramouse Dona Cooper has a special place where her grandchildren have always gone as soon as they hit the door—an area of the den in front of a big picture window. There are toys, a little table, books—they can touch everything there. Now the great-grandchildren are drawn to that same area!!

There are dress-up clothes in that area—jewelry, shoes, frilly nighties, hats, purses. "It encourages creativity, imagination—they can be anyone!" Dona reports that one of the little ones would start taking off her clothes the moment she walked in the door and went straight to the dress-up area. Dona has written many poems to illustrate this area. One such poem from *Family Ties* –

TOY BOX BOUTIQUE

She chose a dress of pink chiffon.
A hat to top her curls.
A purse of patent leather.
A strand of finest pearls.
White gloves, and diamond bracelets
To dangle from each sleeve,
Then wobbled off in blue high heels
To a world of make-believe.

Nan Georgan's granddaughter, Avery Anne, now 3 ½, loves dressing up in anything! Shoes, old fur collars, necklaces—all are special to her! Georgan bought her a Cinderella costume, and her reaction—"It is itchy, but I just love it!"

Nan's grandson, Reagan, now 5, loves Legos. She confesses that she made the mistake of letting him pick out a special Lego set to play with during a week-long visit. "After I tried for over three hours to put it together, I read on the side of the box, '8-16 year-olds'! It remains in a special place under the guest bed for future visits!" (See Appendix B for age-appropriate toys and games for children.)

Gramma Bev, who has the good fortune of living in the shadow of the Grand Tetons in Wyoming, says "When my grandchildren come to visit, what we enjoy most is nature and the outdoors. We walk in the woods or along a lake or creek, listening for nature's sounds— the call of a Sandhill crane, the song of a tiny yellow warbler or even the dramatic bugle of a big bull elk!"

"Over the years the favorite activity of nearly all of our ten grandchildren has been an excursion to Pacific Creek near our home. What they enjoy most is kicking off their shoes and wading in the cold water, digging and playing in the warm sand, and skipping rocks on the water."

Although visits from grandsons in Seattle are rare for Honna Judy in Edmond, Oklahoma, they enjoy going to the playground, singing songs in the car, cooking—especially baking cookies - having tea parties, and sleeping with Honna in her room. "The favorite activity for these two 'busy' boys is playing outside, riding bikes or scooters and going to the zoo."

For Grammar Pat, the thing she enjoys most when the grandchildren come to visit is "kissing them over and over, asking questions, laughing at their answers, and listening as they sprinkle in their own laughter." She plays Wa-Hoo (a board game) with Jack, age 5, and the pre-schoolers like to paint, practice the letters of the alphabet, work puzzles, and play a game of "Old Maid".

"A special treat for all of them is a visit to Barnes & Noble, where, if we aren't careful, we have ransacked the children's area and leave with $100 worth of 'must have' books!" When she asked the 8-year-old and 4-year-old what they enjoyed the most at her house, they replied enthusiastically, "Riding the tractor with Pops, painting, piling up with a bowl of popcorn to watch movies, and playing Chinese checkers!"

Momo Suzanne, who is blessed to have all of her grandchildren in the same town, enjoys spending time with them individually. They play outside, watch the birds, and they often spend the night. They also read and play games, but she admits that "Grandpa's games are better, because he's a little rougher." I know, too, that Suzanne entertains them with sing-alongs, while she plays her ukulele.

When grandchildren come to visit Diane Coffey's house in Stillwater, Oklahoma, "Breakfast is big!" Sometimes "Dinah" serves it in the kitchen/breakfast area, where they have a TV/video combo; sometimes in the "Rabbit Room"–so named because of the huge white bunnies in the wallpaper. While Dinah allows her daughters to sleep in (something rare for them!), she prepares all of the grandchildren's favorite items– pancakes with mini-chocolate chips and powdered sugar–mounds of it! waffles and French toast; Malt-o-Meal, oatmeal, sausage, bacon and eggs!!

Her grandchildren—all 13 of them—LOVE to be with their cousins!! They have the *most* fun when others are there. The more the merrier! One day when little Cooper came to visit, he went through the entire house and finding no cousins present, he said to Dinah "Where are all my friends?"

Dinah says that her grandchildren (ages 5 to 10) love to make hideouts in the Rabbit Room—with lots of sheets and clothespins. They love tea parties at daughter Emily's old table. They like to pretend, but LOVE the real thing!! Even serving water is fun—and it cleans up easily!

They enjoy the outdoors too. They love to jump on the trampoline with Dinah, and they beg her to go swimming with them. They call out, "Is it beauty shop day?!" because they know that if it is, she will make the plunge. Recently they bought a horse. Their 5-year-old grandson, Cooper, wanted a horse more than anything, so they keep a horse nearby for all of the grandchildren to ride.

Grammie Linda Black, whom I met on a plane on the way to Phoenix, AND whose interview I wrote on the back of a "barf bag", said that what her grandson, Jackson, 5 ½, enjoyed most was playing make-believe about everything! "Everything has a name—their cars are "Freddie Forerunner' and 'Teddy Trooper'." His teddy bears all have names, and she uses it as a teaching tool. They talk about everything he is playing with. "Jackson loves trains! He loves *Thomas the Train* stories, and we make-believe the trains need repair, and we talk about how to do an oil change."

Mom Betty has had to share her grandsons over the years with "Pop" Larry. They would "help" him run errands in his '55 Chevy with James Brown rock 'n roll on the "before-stereo" radio. Their favorite activity was to spend the night–one at a time. On these overnights they played "Bear" (rough-housing) with Pop and cards or games with Mom Betty. At bedtime, each had his own special pillowcase–Donald, Mickey, and Pluto–one side awake, the other asleep.

Grammie Linda Black pointed out that they avoid two things–TV and the computer. Since her grandson experiences these at home, they try to do things that are different. He loves the snow, so they play in it–sometimes for hours at a time–and he never wants to come in! They make snow buildings, bury each other in the snow, and make BIG snow forts with 5-gallon buckets–as well as sledding and snowmobiling.

Grammar Pat Downs lets the grandchildren help plant a vegetable garden. "Digging potatoes is the most fun!" Pat and her husband, Billy Red, also have an improvised "hayride" for their grandchildren. Grandpa pulls them around their 2 ½ acres with his tractor. What could be more fun??!!

Carol Headrick's grandchildren must count the days between visits to their Grandmother's house!! When grandchildren come to visit Grandmother Carol, they have a real treat in store!! They do some of the traditional things–playing games, doing projects, and having tea parties–with real tea and treats, of course. BUT that's not all!!

She has a mail box for each one, where she puts notes, pictures, and small gifts. When they arrive for a visit, they run to check the mailboxes for their surprises. You can put up the flag to indicate, "You've got mail!"

They also set the table each day sometimes with stemmed glasses and lighted candles. (She even has a snuffer!) They enjoy cooking simple things like making bread sticks out of hot dog buns, and each one has a turn at being hostess, so they can practice their manners. Spills are not a problem, but they *must* respect each other—no interrupting or competition.

They especially enjoy playing with the games their parents played with, but their favorite game is "Hiding in the Dark". One goes to hide; the others begin their search, talking as they go. When one finds the person, they stop talking. "When they are small, they stick close to me, but as they get older, they become quite brave!"

"They love digging for worms and fishing in the creek behind our house. In winter they will sled for hours, and snow walks are fun, too—following tracks of birds, rabbits, and squirrels." They make igloos together, and when they go in, pulling hot taffy in buttered hands is sure to warm them up! "It involves all of the senses—a tradition I think they will remember."

Bedtime is another thing they're not likely to forget! "BEDTIME MUST BE GOOD!" Carol insists. She climbs in bed with them, and they share scary stories. What a perfect way to end the day! What fun memories for these lucky grandchildren!!

Some of the grandmas with older children shared their ideas–

Mema Lois's grandchildren like to come for overnights. "My teenage granddaughters call it 'Girls' Night Out'. In summer time we spend time in the swimming pool at my condominium complex. Then we have some of their favorite foods like pizza and root beer floats. We top the evening off with a favorite video or movie." Lois, like many other grandmas, also reported that they enjoyed playing board games and cards with their older grandchildren.

Gram Mary says that now that her grandchildren are older, they spend a lot of time just visiting. "They are a very interesting and busy group with a wide range of talents, and I love to hear their thoughts about anything and everything–their thoughts about their futures–their dreams." Certainly children of ALL ages value a listener!

Grams Mary Anne, who has been a wonderful athlete over the years, loves to play tennis with her grandchildren. While they were growing up, she had a paddleball court at her house, and we remember fondly the family tourneys to which we were invited. She also enjoys playing cards, cooking for them and reading with them. She regularly attends their athletic events and is a big fan!

Chapter Four

STORY TIME WITH GRANDMA!

How can we impart a love for reading to our grandchildren?

How can we help them become avid readers?

Certainly, reading stories with your grand-children is a "no-fail" activity!! They love the beautiful books, but just as much, they love the attention, the closeness, the cuddling. I think they love that you are staying in one spot–not running around doing chores like their moms have to do. When they are young, they love to read the same books over and over! There is security in repetition, and they may begin to recognize familiar words.

Reading research confirms that reading rhymes to children increases their success with phonics (which is back *en vogue*!), and helps them to become more proficient readers. Reading is absolutely essential to a child's success in school–and life. What a wonderful opportunity we have to help ensure this success! How can we do this?

Here are some secrets for making story time memories:

1. Find your "special" places to read–in a rocker, under a "tent" made from a quilt or sheet draped over a card table. Read on the porch swing, on a blanket under a tree, or in the park. It might even be fun to read a scary story in a closet with a flashlight! Let them know that reading can be fun! Since many parents read to them each night, sometimes they associate reading with bedtime and shy away from it, thinking that they will have to go to sleep at the end of story time. Help dispel this myth! Reading is great fun *anytime!*

2. Introduce them to the world of books at the library. Almost every library has a story time and other activities to encourage a child's interest in reading. What fun to select books together to take home! In addition to enhancing their love for books, they become aware of the many resources available at the library.

3. Take them to your local bookstore. They always have a great children's section with the latest books, and large bookstores often have story time and other activities as well. Perhaps a children's author will entertain the children and sign one of her books for them! Check with your bookstore for a calendar of events.

4. Tell them stories!! My mother loved telling stories to her grandchildren, and my dear Aunt Lucy was "Grandma" to our daughters after my mother died. She continued the "tickle-back" tradition with them, as she had done with us. The routine was the same. She would lie down with them on the sofa-bed, and they would take turns "tickling backs" while she

created "yarns" or stories, often with them as the main characters. They would want the same stories told over and over, and I marvel at how she could remember, since they were always "off the top of her head".

As I now try to mimic this wonderful tradition with my own grandchildren, I appreciate her "gift" more and more. The "tickling" may well have been a ploy to get us to sleep, but for us, it's a wonderful memory of a fantastic storyteller!

5. Listen to stories on records and follow along in the book. Make a recording of your reading a book, and play it back with your grandchild. Honna Judy Morrison, who lives 2,000 miles from her grandchildren, buys a book, makes a cassette tape of her reading it; then sends both to her grand-boys. They love it! They get to hear their grandmother's voice and subtly discover that reading is fun! As they get older, encourage them to make tapes of their own reading and send to you!

6. Let them "read" to you! There is nothing more important to a child's success in school OR in life than knowing how to read! The earlier they learn, the more practice they receive, and the faster they read. The faster they read, the more they enjoy it and the more they learn. The more they learn, the more accomplished they are, and the more recognition they receive. With recognition comes self-esteem and confidence.

In my opinion, a young child learns best through phonics and "tracking"–that is, following along with him as he reads, sounding out words as you go along. Our daughter's first grade teacher told her she would "cut off her fingers" if she caught her "tracking" because she thought it would slow her down at a time when "sight-reading" was the "in" thing. When a child is first learning to read, however, placing your finger under the word to be read, sounding it out when necessary, helps him to focus on the words to be read. Sometimes, it's even good to expose only the word he is focusing on, as it is often intimidating to the beginning reader to see a whole line of words!

It is virtually impossible for a teacher with 20-25 students to teach in this way. Each child must practice outside the classroom, and the grandmother can help in this way to improve the child's reading skills. By age 3 or 4, the children can begin to read to Grandma–very simple books with few words. As the book gets longer, it is fun to take turns–Grandma reads a page, then the child reads the next. As they get a little older, you may want to offer rewards for the number of books they read with you or their parents.

7. Write stories with them OR have them tell you stories, and you write them down. If more than one child is with you, have each child add a sentence on to the story you have begun. This is fun and creative, and they can take it home to Mom and Dad. As they get older, you might want them to illustrate the book, put in a ribbon binding, etc. They can become authors!

Grammar Pat Downs writes books with her grandchildren, beginning at the age of three. When they come to visit, each child has a book he/she "works" on. Pat suggests what they might want to draw a picture of the family, a picture of a trip they've made, a picture of a holiday, a picture of a school activity, etc. Each child creates a book each year and gives it to the parents for Christmas.

> "When each grandchild turns three, we begin "writing" books together. Throughout the year we talk about important events and then illustrate each page, using colorful magic markers. We have drawings of birthday cakes, fireworks, tractors, and families–everything imaginable! This is a gift to their mothers at Christmas time. Debbie (Pat's daughter) reports that Jack and Zeke's are 'tear-stained treasures'!"

She orders the blank books from Tree Top Publishing, (1-800-255-9228 or www.barebooks.com) I ordered some myself–only $1.40 each with no shipping or handling charges!! What a deal!! The covers are white, so they can be personalized, or they have a variety of cover designs to select from.

Ideas From Other Grandmas
on how they have helped develop a love for reading in their grandchildren

Nan Georgan shares, "I have 'read-along' books with audio tapes in my car, which they enjoy reading over and over again. The rule at Nan's house is that we read a book before we watch a Disney video. No complaints!"

Many grandmothers give books for gifts–birthdays, graduation (after *each* school year!), Christmas, Valentine's Day, St. Patrick's Day, Easter, July 4, spring, summer, fall, winter–in other words, books make any day special!! Grandmother "Dinah" gives books according to the grandchildren's interests. "Each grandchild now has a collection!"

Grandma Mary Ostlund's grandchildren have always loved to read, and she keeps "coffee table" books and books of interest in their bedrooms, which they enjoy.

Grandmother Carol Headrick makes up stories with her grandchildren. They can write stories or simply tell them to Carol, who types them. Then they act out the stories. They sometimes do "add-on" stories, which are fun while traveling in the car. She can begin a story; then each child will take turns adding a sentence. She also encourages them to read by sending letters containing articles of interest for each child. When they are small, try writing them simple letters in block print and ask them to read the letters to their parents.

Momo Suzanne Carpenter writes and illustrates books for and about her grandchildren, laminating the pages, so they can be treasures for years.

Some of Lois Brewster's grandchildren are home schooled, so she enjoys going over once a week to help them with their reading. "When they have gotten to the point where they can read 75 three-letter phonetic words in 3 minutes and know a few of the sight words, they begin reading simple books to me. Then I read to them. We set intermediate goals. When they reach a goal, they get a treat which is $1.50 spent at a candy store or placed in their banks. The number of books required for a treat gets less as they get older, as the books take longer to read."

NOTE: All the grandmothers agreed that one of the very best ways to encourage a love for reading in our grandchildren is to let them see us reading! In a world dominated by television, this is a challenge!

Favorite Books

Many of the grandmothers join me in sharing our "favorite books" to read with our grandchildren:

Bible storybooks:
The Bible in Pictures for Little Eyes,
Kenneth N. Taylor

Arch Books (rhyming Bible stories–paperback)

Baby's First Bible (board book), Muff Singer

Baby's First Nativity (board book), Muff Singer

The First Christmas (pop-up book), Tomie de Paola

The Story of Easter for Children, Ideals Publishing

When Jesus Comes to My House

The Bible for Children (simplified Bible text)

3 in 1: A Picture of God, Marxhauser

Books our children and grandchildren love:

Nursery Rhyme books

Mother Goose

Fairy Tales

Dr. Seuss books

Disney books

Winnie the Pooh books

Clifford books

Curious George books

Little Critter books

Corduroy books

Raggedy Ann books

Madeline books

Amelia Bedelia books

Garden of Verses, Stevenson

Golden Books–Classics

Golden Shape Books–*Telephone Book, Farm Book, House Book, Puppy Book,*

Clock Book, Circus Book, etc.

Good Dog, Carl - Day

Little Black, A Pony

Harry, the Dirty Dog

Little Bear books, Elsie Minarik

The Little Engine that Could, Piper

Frog and Toad Together, Lobel

The Snowy Day, Keats

Something is Coming (Lift the Flap book), Chardiet

My Mother is the Most Beautiful Woman in the World, Reyher

Mommies at Work, Merrian

The Pumpkin Blanket, Zagwyn

Favorite authors:

Patricia Polacco–*Babushka's Doll, Babushka Baba Yaga, Thundercake*

Judith Viorst–*Rosie and Michael, Alphabet Z to A; If I were in Charge of the World, I'd Fix Anthony; Alexander and the Terrible, Horrible, No Good, Very Bad Day*

Charlotte Zolotow–*Big Brother; Big Sister and Little Sister; Do You Know What I'll Do? I Know a Lady; Mr. Rabbit and the Lovely Present; One Step, Two; Sleepy Book; The Storm Book; The Sky was Blue; Hold My Hand*

Eric Carle–*The Hungry Caterpillar, The Foolish Tortoise, My Apron, The Very Busy Spider*

Aliki–*My Five Senses, Feelings*

Millicent Selsam–*Terry and the Caterpillars, Seeds and More Seeds, Benny's Animals,* and other children's science books

Tomie de Paola–*The Knight and the Dragon, The Legend of the Bluebonnets, The Legend of the Poinsettia, The Christmas Story (pop-up) ,The Quilt Story*

Richard Scarry–word books

Books to Encourage:
Helen Keller

The Young Patriot Series–Children's Biographies (Heroes and Heroines)

The Little Engine that Could, Piper

Somebody Loves You, Mr. Hatch–Spinelli

Will I Have a Friend? Cohen

Johnny Appleseed, tale retold by Kellogg

The Tortoise and the Hare, Aesop

The Shy Little Girl, Krasilovsky

Today I Feel Silly, Curtis

Books on Death:

> *The 10 Good Things about Barney*
> (death of a pet), Judith Viorst

> *Badger's Parting Gifts*, Susan Varley

> *The Worry Stone*, Marianne Dengler

> *A Taste of Blackberries*, Doris Buchanan Smith

> *The Fall of Freddie the Leaf*, Leo Buscaglia

Favorite Cookbook for Children:

> *Betty Crocker's Cookbook for Boys and Girls*

NOTE: For a more extensive list of recommended books according to age and interest, see Appendix B.

Chapter Five

LEARNING FROM GRANDMA

$\mathcal{T}$here is nothing more fun that "helping" Grandma!! Every grandchild can learn from watching Grandma do her "chores" and participating with her. She becomes a mentor to the child and is able to "take the time" to teach when "readiness" is at its peak–when the child *wants* to learn!!

1. Cook together. If you are making a pie, have a small pan for them to use in making one, too. Make and decorate cookies together for the holidays. Make pancakes with faces or in shapes like Mickey Mouse. Make drop biscuits for breakfast and scrambled eggs. They love to break the eggs and stir! Make a fun and nourishing salad with them.

Make miniature pizzas with refrigerated biscuits and a variety of toppings. Make "pigs in the blanket" wrapping biscuits around cocktail sausages. Use cookie cutters to cut shapes from bread–then spread with peanut butter and make banana and/or raisin faces. Make Jello and pour into animal molds, or make instant pudding and serve with animal crackers for dessert.

Or do something as simple as chocolate milk, letting them add chocolate syrup to milk and stirring it. Just doing these things together makes it fun!

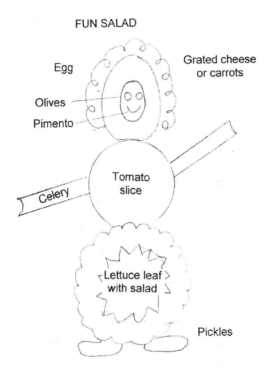

FUN SALAD

Egg

Grated cheese or carrots

Olives

Pimento

Tomato slice

Celery

Lettuce leaf with salad

Pickles

2.   Garden together—God will surely bless the little seedling that is plopped into the ground by the chubby little hands of a child.   AND there's nothing like harvesting a crop of tomatoes, carrots, radishes, peppers, green beans or strawberries!   What fun to help Grandma snap peas or green beans, put them in a pot with some bacon and water, and eat them at dinner!

3. Learn about saving money–give them a bank; let them earn money for doing small chores. Be sure the task is within their abilities, so it will be fun. As they get older, teach them about investments. You may even want to give them a share of stock for their birthdays or at Christmas to peak their interest.

4. Sew together–start with simple doll blankets. You may even want to "glue" clothes together at first! Or sew a little doll or teddy bear together, and let him/her stuff it, draw a face on it, etc. Later, as they are older, you can make things together. There are many simple quilting projects you can do with them.

Grandmother Carol Headrick taught her grandchildren to make quilts! They would go together to select the fabrics they wanted; then Carol would help them cut the squares and put batting between the top and bottom layers. The children would sew an X on the machine, and Carol would sew these squares into quilts.

PATCH QUILT

Children can select a favorite fabric to make a "patch" quilt.
Cut 2 squares for each block, and put batting in the middle.
Mark an "X" on the fabric, and let child sew on the machine.
The size of the quilt will determine the number of blocks.
Grandma can sew the "patches" together later.

They had so much fun with this project, that
they made another type of quilt, this one out of fleece
fabric. Again the children would select 1 ½ yards of
their favorite fabric. Carol would cut out the corners;
then they would cut strips along the edge–4-6 inches
deep. The children would simply tie the strips
together. No batting was needed, because the fleece
fabric was so soft and cuddly.

FLEECE BLANKET

Use two pieces of fleece fabric – 1 ½ yards each.
(One with pattern; the other plain)

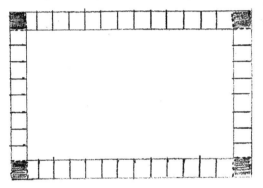

Cut 4" up on each side to form 1" strips.
Cut out the corners and tie strips together
to form "fringe".

5. Do "Hand Work" together–My grandmother was
the one who taught me how to embroider and do a
simple "cross stitch" project. What a blessing that has
been over the years!! Begin with a very simple pattern
and large count cloth. (They can see much better than
we can! BUT it is easier for them to handle a larger
cloth, larger needle, etc.) Have a fun goal–making

something for Mom or Dad!   Have them embroider their names or "I love you, Mom", using simple back stitching and satin stitching for the heart. Be sure to tie a little knot at the needle's eye, so the thread will not slip out.

Although learning a variety of skills from Grandma is very important, perhaps far more important are the values they can learn from us. Grandmothers have the wisdom of age and experience, and grandchildren–even teenage grandchildren–are perhaps not as resistant to advice from grandparents as they are from their parents.

Grandmother "Dinah" Coffey gives advice to her grandchildren–but always with humor. "There is no power struggle like there might be with Mom or Dad." She begins with "Oh, honey" . . . then gives the "lecture"; then says, "Lecture's over!" She tries to be available to all thirteen grandchildren equally.

Diane tries to give them lots of approval and encouragement. "I learned this from my father. He would say to his granddaughters, 'You are the cutest thing I've ever seen!' He was sincere, and they believed it. I need to let them know how wonderful they are." She tries to stay tuned into what each child needs. "Hugs are important! A hug plus 'You're the best!' goes a long way in healing wounds or making up for losses in a child's life."   (A friend refers to these hugs as "Vitamin H"! Perfectly said.)

Grandma Lou Watkins, wife of long-time U. S. Congressman Wes Watkins, is a very active grandparent

to her grandchildren who live close to her on Peaceable
Acres in Stillwater, Oklahoma, where each of their three
children has an acre on which to rear the grandchildren.
Every summer Lou holds "Grandma School" for her
school-age grandchildren.   At the beginning of the
summer she talks with each child and determines his/her
needs and interests and comes up with a list of activities
which will make up the child's summer program.

Grandma Lou took advantage of the activities
offered in the Stillwater community for grandchildren,
Bradley, Beth, and Rena for Grandma School, 2005:

YMCA swimming lessons
OSU basketball camp
Stillwater Library's Summer Reading Program
Watercolor lessons at the Multi-Arts Center
Kids Fitness Zone Summer Olympics
Stillwater Diamondbacks baseball
Guitar or other music lessons
Cheernastics at OSU Cowboy Kids
Bible School
"Play Days" at OSU Rodeo Grounds

The activities were individualized.   For example,
Bradley helped his dad with the cattle, while Beth
helped her mom in the kitchen and around the house.
They both attended a family reunion in Indiana,
while Rena went to Colorado with her parents.   Beth
biked around Boomer Lake to support her mom's MS
Walk, and Rena attended a barrel-racing clinic in Ada,
Oklahoma.

At the end of the summer Lou has a Graduation Program and dinner to help celebrate their accomplishments. The children help her plan the evening and participate in it. They welcome guests, lead the pledge to the flag, and offer the blessing on the food. The children tell "What I Did and Liked best in Grandma School", and then Grandma Lou presents the decorative diplomas. The evening's festivities close with their leading the family in singing "God Bless America". What a wonderful tradition and legacy for her grandchildren!! Youngest grandchild, Emma, now 3, is already looking forward to it!

Dorothy Carter, former first lady of Gillette, Wyoming, would applaud Lou's efforts in teaching her grandchildren the value of an education. She has been a strong voice in that community to ensure it has the finest schools. Her grandchildren also have learned the importance of public service from her and, at a young age, are following her example and contributing to their communities.

Mema Lois Brewster hopes her 12 grandchildren are learning important values like trust. "I want them to know that they can depend on me; that I am always here for them; that I will always level with them–I will tell the truth. I want them to learn that it is very important that *they* live in such a way that others can trust *them*. I see this as an integral part of the unconditional love that should be shared in families."

Grandma Mary Ostlund, hopes that her grandchildren are learning about the joy of commitment–commitment to the love of God, to country, to a spouse, and to a healthy lifestyle—by example, not just by words or preaching. "I fly the American flag every day in appreciation for our country. I think they have learned how great it is to live in the United States."

Grandmother Carol Headrick hopes that her grandchildren are learning to listen to others and be sensitive to their needs. She has encouraged them to imagine—to role-play—to show emotion. She also wants them to have good manners.

"Dinah" Coffey points out that she makes her grandchildren mind! She is permissive unless there is a standing rule against it. No sass! When she tells them to do something, she expects them to do it. She has, on occasion, even spanked. She observes, "I grandparent like my mother. She made us mind. I remember the green ruler! But we loved her dearly! We think our grandchildren are adorable, but we must discipline them so others will think so too!"

Grandma Anita Ibison hopes her grandchildren will learn to trust in God, to have fun in life, and to know that she loves them unconditionally. Her friend and mine, Judy Morrison, hopes that her grandsons know that they are accepted and valued for who they are and know that she loves them completely.

Momo Suzanne Carpenter hopes her grandchildren are learning humor! "Josh is so serious, so it is fun to make him giggle—I try to teach him to laugh at himself, but it doesn't always work. On a trip to Chicago, Josh, who was six, rode on the elevator. When it stopped, she got right out, but Josh stayed on. When she caught up with him, she said, "Josh, someday we'll laugh at this." He replied, "Momo, this will *never* be funny!"

Gramma Bev Babcock, who lives in beautiful Wyoming, wants her grandchildren to honor God and to appreciate God's creation in nature. She also has tried to teach her grandchildren gratitude! If someone does something nice, you should thank him! A very simple but important lesson!

Although Gramouse Dona has made "millions" of cookies with her grandchildren–decorating them and licking the spoon–she hopes she is remembered as one who has written down and preserved their family's history. "It's important for them to understand the family to fully understand and appreciate who they are as persons." Dona has done this so beautifully through her poetry and by encouraging the telling of stories around the table–"Remember when . . .".

Grandmother Carol Headrick, too, senses the need for grandparents to be "providers of family history". "We must see that they become acquainted with the great grandparents–visit them, hear stories about them, understand their heritage." They have taken their grandchildren to see Carol's mother. They took pictures of them by her house and allowed time for the children to ask questions.

Grams Mary Anne Price hopes her 16 grandchildren are learning to be respectful, thankful, polite, and loving. That just about sums up every grandmother's desires.

Although the primary responsibility for teaching these values belongs to the parents, grandparents can reinforce these lessons. And in a day when often both parents work, the need for that is greater than ever. Grandchildren should know that

1. they are loved unconditionally by their family and God
2. they must respect differences in people
3. they should listen to others
4. they have strengths and weaknesses
5. they must never stop learning, and
6. they should see that learning is an adventure!

We can teach these lessons by setting an example, by role-playing, using analogies, games, story books, and encouraging them to risk–try different things, welcome adventure, look forward to trying new things. It is important, however, to expose them to things that are age-appropriate or ability-appropriate. When we try something beyond their developmental abilities, we are setting them up to fail. We want them to be *successful*!!

Chapter Six

HOLIDAYS WITH GRANDMA

Christmas

I don't have many holiday memories with my grandmothers to draw from. We were very poor, so holidays were simple. We always had Christmas at home–once with an evergreen tree Daddy cut from our small back yard! My Grandma Acosta from Louisiana was never with us, and I remember only an occasional visit from my Grandma Mellie when we were small. She seemed to enjoy the Christmas Eve program we prepared and presented for them, and she made us feel like movie stars!! I can only tell you what I have done and plan to do with my grandchildren, AND my grandma friends have lots of ideas to share!!

1. Let your grandchildren help you decorate the Christmas tree!! OR create a grandchild tree, using very special ornaments the children have created! Enjoy making paper loop garlands, bells or stars with the child's photo at the center, or paper cones with greenery and berries. Use lots of glitter!! Listen to Christmas carols while you're engaged in any holiday activity!

2. Making a nativity using old clothespin figures and a cardboard creche will allow you to share the "real" meaning of Christmas. Use an Advent calendar to create anticipation and excitement about the birth of Jesus. Have a birthday party for Him! Make Him a cake!

3. Make a "cookie tree" for the kitchen! Cut out cookies, using your old Christmas cutters–stars, bells, candy canes, Santa, angels, lambs, donkeys, camels, packages, snowflakes, gingerbread men/women, etc. Poke a hole in the top of each before baking; add hanger after they've cooled. Later invite Mom and Dad or friends for cookies and hot chocolate, and take the cookies right off the tree!!

4. Invite your grandchildren, family, and friends to go Christmas caroling in the evening, and invite everyone over for Christmas cookies and hot chocolate afterward! Share stories of favorite Christmas memories. This will help the children see the impact of family traditions.

5. Go see the Christmas lights!! Just a simple drive through your neighborhood or in other parts of town noted for their lights and decorations is such a fun activity for children!! In the Tulsa area, families have a very special opportunity to enjoy the incredible lights of Rhema Bible College. Thousands of lights!! It is a favorite activity for our grandchildren!!

6. Church Christmas programs and pageants are a "must see" for the grandchildren!! Many large churches have great child-friendly programs and celebrate the Christmas story with live animals, which are intriguing

to children. Some churches have a "Living Christmas Tree", where choir members form a tree and sing wonderful Christmas music. Of course, you'll want to attend Christmas programs where your grandchildren are the "stars", as they get older.

7. Take advantage of special Christmas activities in your area. Near Pryor, Oklahoma, many in the area enjoy the Christmas Train at "Dry Gulch, USA". The Bible story from creation to the birth of Jesus is told through beautiful scenes along the tracks, and there are wagon rides, other fun activities, and places to eat or have cookies and hot chocolate.

In Chickasha and Ponca City, Oklahoma–there are wonderful Christmas light celebrations. In smaller communities they often have Christmas parades. That tradition is available here in Stillwater, Oklahoma. We go to the holiday exhibit at the Sheerar Museum and enjoy refreshments there at 5:00pm; then we walk two blocks to a favorite kid-friendly restaurant for dinner, then watch the annual Christmas Parade, A memorable evening!

8. The Mall in a larger city is the center of much holiday activity, and grandchildren can enjoy the window decorations, listen to Christmas music, ride a train or carousel, and sit on Santa's lap. You can shop for parents and friends while you're there. Teach them to shop for "bargains".

9. It's fun to watch one of the classic Christmas films with your grandchildren. *Miracle on 34th Street, Holiday Inn, What a Wonderful Life* are just a few "oldies" we have enjoyed watching with our

grandchildren. Pop some popcorn to make the evening complete.

10.   Our favorite Christmas activity with our grandchildren is to read the Christmas story from Luke 2:1-19–with a "twist". Before the reading, we pass out pieces of the Nativity set, which have been wrapped as gifts–just in tissue is fine. The children and other family members unwrap their "treasures", and as the story is read, they place their pieces in the creche at the appropriate time. For example, as you read verse 4, "So Joseph also went up from the town of Nazareth in Galilee . . .", the child holding "Joseph" would place him in the creche.

This is a family tradition, which makes the story of Christ's birth come to life. It made it "real" for our children. In fact, when our daughter, Stefanie, was four, she added to the creche all of her plastic farm animal figures!

IDEAS FROM OTHER GRANDMAS!

Nana Betty Tower holds an annual Gingerbread House competition in her cozy dining room. Her three "grandsons", now teenagers, have participated with the whole family since they were very young, and now her little granddaughters take part in what is a tradition that bridges the generation gap. Each "contestant", seated around the table, is given a house and one reindeer made of graham crackers. Icing of every color and a variety of decorations are provided to help them design their own. All have fun, and it really doesn't matter who "wins" the competition!

Betty also has recorded her family history with her "photo album" tree! Located on the hearth is a tree covered with photo ornaments of family members at different ages. What fun to reminisce! The grandchildren know that they are cherished–now and at every age in the past!

Gramma Bev, our dear church family friend who now lives in the Grand Tetons National Park, loves Christmas because of the many "warm and wonderful family traditions". For example, each Christmas she hides an almond in the Christmas rice pudding, which is shared at breakfast on Christmas morning. Whoever finds the almond in his/her serving will get to pass out the gifts.

To answer the dilemma of "where to spend Christmas", Dona Cooper has the perfect solution! For "Gramouse" Dona (whose eight grandchildren were born in seven consecutive years!) it doesn't matter which day you celebrate Christmas with the family– any day during the holidays when everyone can get together works fine!

After a scrumptious meal (I know her cooking!!), the family gathers around the tree for a talent show. Cathy plays banjo, Nat plays guitar–everyone does something! "Grandmother always makes us do something!" is the happy "complaint". Dona reads one of the previous Christmas poems, which have become the family's history, and Don reads the Christmas story from the 1857 family Bible–a big leather one, very worn! It's clear that the lessons from The Book have been passed down through this wonderful family!

"Momo" Suzanne Carpenter celebrates Advent with her grandchildren. All of the cousins come over to her house each week to light the candles and review the symbols of the Advent season. This helps remind the children, and everyone in the family, of the "reason for the Season".

Karen Gallagher reads the book, *Too Many Toys* to her grandchildren. This is a beautiful story of a young boy who has so many toys that he can't walk in his room or sleep in his bed. It tells of the wonderful way he solves this problem by piling Santa's sleigh high with his abundance to take to children who are less fortunate. Karen hopes to help them become aware of the joy in giving and the burden of having too many "things". (The lesson was not wasted on her older friends, as she shared the book with us as well!!)

Grandmas can help the children shop for parents, siblings, and friends–encouraging the "giving" aspect and love which should be shared at Christmas. They can *make* gifts with the children and even the wrappings. A favorite activity is stretching plain white wrapping on the floor, putting hands or feet in paint (or brushing paint onto the hands and feet) and decorating the paper with these treasured symbols. Never overlook an opportunity to show the grandchildren how they can save money by doing things themselves!

Grandma Mary Ostlund says that her grandchildren enjoy listening to her tales of "the old days". These memories are shared on special holiday occasions, when everyone dresses up and dines out or comes to her house.. These occasions are always big gatherings–Mary has eight children and eight grandchildren!–and all three generations enjoy each other's company.

Some grandmas, like Grandmother Carol Headrick, think that holidays are not the *best* time to spend with grandchildren because the "Holidays are hectic, and it's not a good time to interact with grandchildren". She agrees, however, that grandchildren may benefit, as they observe the interactions of the family, giving the children a sense of security that comes from being a part of a family.

We can't overestimate the value of traditions for our families!! They offer security, stability, and represent love for our grandchildren, who are constantly bombarded with the fleeting images of 150 channels and the materialism of the world. They look forward to these simple traditions repeated each year at a family gathering and will most likely pass them on to their children and generations to come.

Thanksgiving

Thanksgiving is often overlooked, as we get caught up in the "hub-bub" of Christmas. This dilemma presents a perfect opportunity, however, for grandmas to teach gratitude and thankfulness. I believe that Thanksgiving is a very special time for families to get together to review our country's history, thank God for His many blessings, and to share our bounty with others. Giving thanks is a very important lesson which we are privileged to teach them.

Certainly, the history of the Pilgrims and the first Thanksgiving are taught in school, but it bears repeating, as we celebrate the holiday in our homes with our families. For many, Thanksgiving is a day when we all get together to share a "feast". We prepare traditional foods–turkey, dressing, cranberry sauce, pumpkin and pecan pies, among other "family favorite" dishes–and it can be an opportunity to establish other traditions as well.

In our family, we gather before the meal, and Mimi Toni reads a short children's book on Thanksgiving. Someone then reads Psalm 100, the Psalm of Thanksgiving. (When I was a child, we memorized Psalm 100 and repeated it together. Perhaps this is something grandmothers could undertake with the children!) When we sit down at the table, we hold hands, as Papa Bill gives thanks for our wonderful feast, our many blessings, too numerous to count! Table conversation is fun and focuses on what we are thankful for. Each person must tell at least two things for which he/she is thankful, and why, in order to "earn" dessert!!

Another table tradition worth considering is one observed by Pat Downs and her family. Grammar Pat is concerned, like many modern grandmas, that our grandchildren don't fully appreciate the many blessings we have as Americans, so she puts on each plate five kernels of corn, representing what the Pilgrims had to eat during their first winter in America. She then reads the poem, "Five Kernels of Corn".

FIVE KERNELS OF CORN

T'was the year of the famine in Plymouth of old,
The ice and the sleet from the thatched roofs had rolled;
West winds howling, pine branches bending so low,
Maple leaves whirling, mid new flurries of snow.
Regardless, the Pilgrims welcomed each new morn;
There were left but for rations, Five Kernels of Corn.
        Five Kernels of Corn!
        Five Kernels of Corn!
But to Pilgrims a feast was Five Kernels of Corn;
To each one was given Five Kernels of Corn.

A new land was revealed, by daring the wave,
Guided to safety, by the strong and the brave.
Give thanks all ye people, be humble and pray.
A new light is dawning, and Truth leads your way.
Ye have for THANKSGIVING Five Kernels of Corn!
        Five Kernels of Corn!
        Five Kernels of Corn!

Of deeds such as these was a new homeland born,
The Pilgrims did sing of "Five Kernels of Corn".
The new nation gave thanks for Five Kernels of Corn!

To the THANKSGIVING feast bring
YOUR Five Kernels of Corn!

I loved the description of the entire Thanksgiving Day at Grammar Pat Downs house in Edmond, Oklahoma.

"Thanksgiving is our very favorite holiday, as the entire family enjoys a festival-like atmosphere. With so many little children of varying ages, we plan activities that appeal to all of them: going on hayrides, creating placemats for the table, making necklaces to wear; building a Gingerbread house and making Christmas ornaments. We enjoy Bingo, bubble gum contests and sack races. Sometimes we paint birdhouses for the winter.

A very simple but important part of the day is having the children prepare special favors for the Thanksgiving feast. They place five kernels of corn in plastic bags and tie them with ribbon. These are a reminder of how much we have in comparison to the meager portions the Pilgrims survived on. The children place the bags at each place at the table; then we read the poem, 'Five Kernels of Corn'.

The children also make up a play and present it to the adults. The adults play horseshoes and, of course, watch football. Throughout the day, everyone eats and cameras click!"

The grandchildren can be involved in preparations for Thanksgiving in a number of ways. The older ones can be in charge of the table decor—selecting the linens and creating a centerpiece from things Grandma has around the house. The younger ones can make place cards by putting Thanksgiving stickers on index cards, folded in half. One of the children can write the names of the guests on the cards, using fall-colored markers.

Small children might enjoy making placemats for the guests. Help them make "turkey" hand prints on colored paper. Paint one hand with brown paint, and place it on the paper. Add the eyes and waddle to the turkey; then the following anonymous poem, used by school teachers everywhere, can be glued on the mat:

> This isn't just a turkey
> As anyone can see.
> I made it with my hand
> Which is a part of me.
>
> It comes with lots of love
> Especially to say,
> I hope you have a very happy
> Thanksgiving Day!

This would also be a great opportunity for Grandma to teach the children how to set the table and role-play manners to surprise the parents! This can all be done ahead of time–during a pre-Thanksgiving visit with Grandma!

There are many wonderful books about Thanksgiving! You might enjoy reading some of them with your grandchildren:

1. *Sarah Morton's Day* (Scholastic, 1989) tells about a typical day in the life of a Pilgrim girl.

2. *Samuel Eaton's Day* (Scholastic, 1989) tells about a Pilgrim boy's day.

3. *Oh, What a Thanksgiving!* by Steven Kroll (Scholastic, 1988) is about a boy living in contemporary times who imagines what life would be like living with the Pilgrims.

4. *Squanto and the First Thanksgiving* (Scholastic) tells the part that Squanto and the Indians played in the first Thanksgiving.

5. *If You Sailed on the Mayflower in 1620* by Ann McGovern, gives a picture of what life was like during the long voyage and the strength of the Pilgrims.

6. *Turkeys, Pilgrims, and Indian Corn* by Edna Barth (Clarion, 1975) is a wonderful book about the history and customs of Thanksgiving.

All of the grandmothers seemed to agree: "Thanksgiving is a wonderful time to give thanks for life and our blessings, and it gives us an opportunity to teach our grandchildren to count their blessings as well."

EASTER

Easter is another favorite holiday for children!! As grandparents, we have a wonderful opportunity to share with our grandchildren the "real story of Easter". Children need to understand the story behind the Easter symbols. What do painted eggs, lilies, rabbits, baby chicks, lambs, new clothes, and even pretzels(!)

have to do with the resurrection of Jesus? They DO—in fact, they have a lot to do with Easter. They are wonderful symbols of the Easter story!

I discovered a book many years ago, which explains clearly the Easter symbols, and I plan to share this with our grandchildren. If your grandchildren are in Sunday School, they perhaps have received this information, BUT we should never take this for granted. In the book *Lilies, Rabbits, and Painted Eggs: The Story of the Easter Symbols,* author Edna Barth traces the history of the Easter symbols in a clear and child-friendly way. She shows how many of them were incorporated into Christianity from early pagan rites, and then were handed down to us as the colorful Easter customs we enjoy today.

As we dye Easter eggs together, see lilies at church, enjoy stroking an Easter rabbit, and wear our new Easter clothes, we can share how these are all symbols of the death and resurrection of Jesus. It would be fun to make little books with our grandchildren, having them draw pictures of the symbols, then pasting beside each a description of why that symbol is important to the Easter story. We could read them together, and they could then share these with their parents and friends.

One grandmother I know became a well-known author of children's books because she wanted her grandchildren to understand the true meaning of Easter. Dorothy Van Woerkom wrote *Stepka and the Magic Fire* and *Wake Up and Listen*, both appropriate books on Easter for older elementary children. Once we understand the true meaning of the symbols, we can have fun using them in our celebration of Easter.

1. Make Easter baskets from construction paper; fill with "grass" and add jelly beans or plastic "eggs". Give to Grandpa, parents, or a friend, OR hiding the eggs in the yard or throughout the house makes for hours of fun!! Remind them that eggs are a symbol of Easter because the baby chick bursts forth from the egg, just as Christ emerged from the tomb.

2. Dye Easter eggs together—few activities are as popular! In the early days of the Church, Christians would decorate the eggs, first with a cross, later with elaborate designs—then would give them to others of the faith, saying "Christ is risen". The recipient would reply, "Christ is risen indeed." What a fun custom to repeat with your grandchildren!

3. Go outside and look for signs of spring—bulbs, tiny leaves, the sun, baby animals, etc. These are all signs of rebirth.   Things that appeared without life—bare trees, flower bulbs—now come to life, just as Christ came forth from the tomb.

4. Make Hot Cross buns together. To make it easy, use canned biscuits, sprinkle with cinnamon, and make a cross of icing on top. Christian monks began baking hot cross buns for the poor 600 years ago, and the English continued the tradition. On Good Friday in England street vendors could be heard shouting,

> "Hot cross-buns, hot cross-buns,
> One a penny, two a penny, hot cross-buns."

5. Grandma Kathy Adams shared a unique recipe for Easter Cookies which you may want to try with your grandchildren:

EASTER STORY COOKIES
–to be made the evening before Easter

You will need:

> 1 cup whole pecans
> 1 teaspoon vinegar
> 3 egg whites
> Pinch salt
> l cup sugar
> Zipper baggie
> Wooden spoon
> Cellophane tape and Bible

Preheat oven to 300 degrees F.

Place pecans in zipper baggie and let children beat them with the wooden spoon to break into small pieces. Explain that after Jesus was arrested, he was beaten by the Roman soldiers. Read John 19:1-3

Let each child smell the vinegar. Put 1 teaspoon vinegar into mixing bowl. Explain that when Jesus was thirsty on the cross, he was given vinegar to drink. Read John 19:28-30.

Add egg whites to vinegar. Eggs represent life. Explain that Jesus gave His life to give us life. Read John 20:10-11.

Sprinkle a little salt into each child's hand. Let them taste it and brush the rest into the bowl. Explain that this represents the salty tears shed by Jesus' followers and the bitterness of our own sin. Read Luke 23:27.

So far the ingredients are not very appetizing. Add 1 cup sugar. Explain that the sweetest part of the story is that Jesus died because He loves us. He wants us to know Him and belong to Him.
Read Psalms 34:8 and John 3:16.

Beat with a mixer on high speed for 12 to 15 minutes until stiff peaks are formed. Explain that the color white represents the purity in the eyes of those whose sins have been cleansed by Jesus. Read Isaiah 1:18 and John 3:1-3.

Fold in broken nuts. Drop by teaspoonfuls onto wax paper-covered cookie sheet. Explain that each mound represented the rocky tomb where Jesus' body was laid. Read Matthew 27:57-60.

Put the cookie sheet in the oven; close the door and turn the oven OFF.

Give each child a piece of tape and seal the oven door. Explain that Jesus' tomb was sealed.
Read Matthew 27:65-66.

GO TO BED! Explain that they may feel sad to leave the cookies in the oven overnight. Jesus' followers were in despair when the tomb was sealed. Read John 16:20 and 22.

On Easter morning, open the oven and give everyone a cookie. Notice the cracked surface and take a bite. The cookies are hollow! On the first Easter Jesus' followers were amazed to find the tomb open and empty.
Read Matthew 28:1-9.

HE IS RISEN!!

6. Make Easter bonnets out of paper plates, artificial flowers, and ribbon. Cut out the center of the plate, color and decorate the "brim" with flowers, and add ribbon. Enjoy Grandma's own Easter Parade! Explain how in "olden days" (first few centuries after Jesus) those who came to know Christ were baptized in water the week before Easter and then put on white robes. Later people dressed in fresh clothing at Easter whether they were newly baptized or not. They took off their winter clothes, bathed in the icy streams, and dressed in their old clothes, which had been freshly washed. After the Easter church service, people dressed in their fresh Easter clothes and went on a special walk together through the town. At certain spots they stopped to pray and sing Easter hymns. Leading the procession was someone carrying a lighted candle, representing Christ, the light of the world. These were the *first* Easter parades.

An Easter parade, of sorts, is held at the home of "Mom" Betty Tower. All of the grandchildren and their parents gather for picture-taking in their Easter "finery". They have the same dinner menu every year, followed by an annual egg toss and Easter egg hunt. Once found, the plastic eggs are opened to reveal funny actions they must do. After much fun and laughter, prizes are awarded. She doesn't let them get away without taking pictures of the children beside the trees that were planted when they were born.

For "Nan" Georgan Reitmeier of Houston, "Easter is the 'most fun' holiday!" Grandpa Tom, "Poppy", has a bunny costume he brings out each year. Together the family watches the children's version of the "Jesus" video, which portrays the life of Jesus leading to the cross.

"Grandma" Mary Ostlund, mother of nine children and grandmother to eight, says that Easter is her favorite too. "It reaffirms our faith in God and the future. It also is the beginning of a new season of spring, which promises sunny days, flowers, budding trees—and time in the outdoors." Anyone who has lived in Wyoming knows the joy of "new life" emerging after the long winters and the beauty of God's creation manifest in that glorious state!

The Easter tradition for "Momo" Suzanne Carpenter is to take her family to the Country Club for Easter Brunch. They sit together at a table which accommodates her three children and their families, which include seven grandchildren, ages two to thirteen.

"Gramouse" Dona Cooper likes to dye, decorate, and hide Easter eggs with her grandchildren. They also hide jelly beans after the Easter dinner—all over the house. With baskets in hand, they begin the hunt. Teasingly, she tells them they must pay ten cents for any jellybean she finds later. As she discovers one while dusting, it serves as a reminder of good times!"

Lois Brewster, who has an even dozen grand-children, says that the three traditions her grandchildren enjoy most, aside from birthday parties, are

1. coloring Easter eggs together. "My 7-year-old grand-daughter said, 'I can't wait for Easter to come so we can color eggs'. We do this on

the patio on newspapers while kneeling on old folded bath towels. Spills always happen, and no one is bothered by that."

2. shucking and freezing corn-on-the-cob together on July 4. Even the tiniest ones can help. Their job is to jump in the trash can when the shucks need to be pressed down.

3. making peanut brittle at Christmas time. All the kids turn out to help when the candy is ready to be stretched on the marble slab.

Certainly, holidays are a great time to celebrate traditions with family. Thanksgiving, Christmas, and Easter are times our grandchildren will always remember—because of the food, the love, the laughter, the games, the gifts, the fun. These holidays hold great lessons about our faith upon which our country and culture were founded.

Chapter Seven

BIRTHDAYS WITH GRANDMA

$\mathcal{P}$robably no day in the life of a child is as important as his birthday! To share in that day's celebration is very special indeed and an opportunity not to be missed if at all possible. When I was young, birthdays were pretty much non-events at my house. Because we were poor, I'm sure they were considered frivolous, so I have no personal memories to draw from in helping my grandchildren celebrate. I do remember going around the neighborhood inviting everyone to my 4th birthday party–a party my mother knew nothing about!! Perhaps this shows how important birthdays are to children!! The following accounts from friends have given me some great ideas to help celebrate our grandchildren's birthdays!

"Mom" Betty Tower makes a special cake for each grandchild. Although a cake decorating class peaked her interest, the subject of each cake was her own creation, depicting what was important to each child that year. Andrew, the teen runner, has enjoyed a cake with a track on it and stick-people "runners"; an earlier cake was shaped like a skateboard, and a more recent one, when he turned 16, was in the shape of car keys.

His younger brother, Matthew, enjoyed a cake with a fallen skier, one shaped like a soccer ball and another like a baseball, depicting his year's activities. Thomas, the youngest, loved his "Game Boy" cake; also a computer screen with "Thomas, you have mail" written on it. When he was 10 years old, there was a dime-shaped cake to go with 10 boxes of his favorite cookies with a $10 bill in each. When he was younger there was a "Big Bird" cake, a rocket cake, a train, and a Ninja Turtle.

When the birthday boy arrives for the celebration, he runs to the table to see the cake. As a background for the cakes, she places all kinds of mementos important to the honoree under the glass on the dining table—"pet" names, photos of the birthday boy or girl, certificates, awards, anything that is important to the child. Then they all eat at that table, talking about and celebrating the life of that grandchild. "Mom" Betty will long be remembered for her love and efforts in creating these memories!

"Mom" Betty is also a master at gift selection– very creative and successful in finding things her grandchildren enjoy. She and "Poppy" Larry encourage their grandsons' outdoor activities with fishing rods or golf clubs from the Orvis catalog. A tent would be another great gift! Clever Grandmother "Suzy" Timberlake's most popular gift for their one-year-old was a very large basket filled with rubber balls– inexpensive lightweight beach type.

Mom and Poppy Tower also put money into an account each birthday and give the birthday child the receipt. They put the grandparent's name on the account, so there will be no problem "begging" parents for the money in the account. When grandson Matthew was 10, they gave him 10 Disney Dollars to announce the family trip to Disneyworld.

"Grandmother" Carol Headrick helps her grandchildren celebrate in a different way. Each child is invited to come along for a visit to do whatever interests him/her. For example, Rebecca wants to be a veterinarian, so when she came for her birthday visit, one of Carol's friends set up a tour of the OSU vet clinic. Carol took pictures, and a neighbor took them to lunch on the OSU campus. They also went to Pawnee to talk with a vet, and Carol took a photo of them together. These and other memories were recorded in words and pictures in a scrapbook about the visit, which was considered by Rebecca, "the BEST gift". This tradition helps each child develop his/her interests and certainly makes each one feel special.

Other grandmothers pen their loving thoughts to their grandchildren. "Grammar" Pat Downs invites the birthday child and family to a special dinner in his/her honor. "Personal archival footage" in the form of a special letter she has written is then read aloud to the birthday grandchild at the dinner table. Karen Gallagher also writes a letter commemorating each of her five grandchildren's birthdays and places it in a plastic sleeve with favorite photos from that year. These pages are placed in a book, which each grandchild can cherish for years to come.

One of my favorite gift ideas comes from Momo Suzanne Carpenter, who writes and illustrates a book with the grandchild as the "main character"– taking into consideration the interests of the child at that time. For example, because there are so many birds in her yard, the children have developed a real interest in birds. In one of her books, *A Bird Book,* each child is a different bird. The child and other family members are pictured in the book as different birds, and the writing reflects what it is about each bird that reminds Momo of the child. These books are laminated and given as gifts to the children.

"Gramouse" Dona Cooper, the author of three published books of poetry, and MANY loose-bound volumes, is providing a wonderful history of the Cooper clan. She writes a poem about each grandchild as a birthday gift. One of the favorites was written for granddaughter Jesse's 16th birthday.

SHIFTING INTO SWEET SIXTEEN

I used to drive you shopping
  When you came to spend the day.
I'd drive you to ballet and school
  When your parents were away.

When you needed a ride to fellowship
  I'd take the chauffeur's seat.
To get you where you had to go
  Was for me a Gramouse treat.

But all too soon those special times
> Have become just memories,
For you now have your driver's license
> And your very own set of keys.

Though I may not be with you in person,
> Please know that my every prayer
Will go with you, Jesse, each mile of the way
> Until you are safely there.

One of Dona's poems memorializes another of her grandchildren, who shall remain unnamed. Her love for "Pampers" is the subject of this clever poem written for her grandchild when she turned three:

PAMPER ME SOME MORE!

Said their "sweetie pie" with sincerity,
"I'll wear panties when I'm three."
And when that day dawned bright and clear,
Rejoiced her mom, "At last it's here."
But then the grandchild we adore
Announced she'd wait 'til she was four.

Dona muses, "Grandchildren are the perfect subject for a Grandmother who is a poet!"   Although I'm not a published poet like Dona, I was inspired by her to write birthday poems for my grandchildren.   Before the birthday, I ask my daughter for highlights of our grandchild's year–school, church, play, activities, friends, etc. Then I write a poem which encompasses all of those things.   I put it on decorative paper, which can be added to the scrapbook our daughter is making for each child.

My husband, "Papa" Bill, thinks I should include one of these birthday poems–perhaps so others can see that "anyone can do it"!

HAPPY BIRTHDAY TO SARA
ON BIRTHDAY #5

"Little Miss Sara", can you believe that she's 5?!
From her, each day, so much pleasure we derive!
"She's such a sweet girl", we all would surely say.
"She's so very thoughtful and kind in every way."

She's had an eventful year since her last birthday;
So many things have happened to her along the way.
A trip to Big Cedar with her whole family in May,
Swimming, hiking, horseback riding–she enjoyed each day!

Another trip to Houston with Mom and Dad in November;
Played with cousins and friends–she'll always remember.
Stayed with Aunt Shellie in her apartment and slept on the floor;
Didn't mind at all–would have loved to have stayed some more!

Visited with Mimi and Papa a number of days–
They love having Sara and Ashley over to play!
These two grandparents love their little Sara girl;
They think she's the best 5-year-old in the whole wide world!

The highlight of the year was the birth of baby brother!
Sara and Ashley think Luke is better than any other.
He loves his sisters, too, and smiles at them all day,
As they are gentle and help him in so many ways.

In her 3rd year at Riverfield Country School
Sara thinks that learning is really "cool".
She helped with the building of "The City of Sounds",
And went on lots of field trips all around town.

Sara's really an artist in a number of ways;
Her drawings are great, and she can work with paint and clay.
She's learned many new songs—she's so smart!
And do you know she's an expert on the monkey bars?!

With other groups she can now communicate—
Her Spanish and sign language skills are first rate!
She's starting to read and understands sounds.
We think she's the most intelligent girl around!

Sara can print her letters and even writes notes.
She wrote one for Luke and put it up on his door.
Sara's teachers say, "She's a joy to have in class."
"Why doesn't that surprise us?" Mimi and Papa ask.

Play Group is fun, and that's for real!
And in SSB she's mastered the cart wheel!
For Christmas she got her very first bike.
And is often seen with her helmet going for a ride.

In church, Sara's in the Pre-K class;
Teacher Brenda enjoys this sweet little "lass".
Vacation Bible School in July was fun for her too.
The SCUBA underwater Bible Adventure was super cool!

Other summer fun included times in the pool,
And water park adventures with Mimi and Papa too.
Sara likes to play games and watch "Veggie Tales".
She enjoys dress up and Barbies and other imaginative play.

She can now make her bed and tie her shoes;
She can brush her teeth and get ready for school.
She can shampoo her hair and get ready for bed;
And to Mom and Dad, some books she has read.

Sara is so helpful, and that makes Jesus happy.
As He sees her help Mom, Baby Luke, and sister Ashley.
Mom and Dad are as proud of their daughter as they can be –
Their precious 5-year-old, SARA GRACE HUMPHREY!

Many grandmothers give money for birthdays–especially as the children get older. "Grandma" Mary Ostlund calls her money gift "Crispies", which are "freshly minted" dollar bills. Her grandmother always sent her "Crispies" in her birthday card, and it was a happy memory she wanted to share with her own grandchildren.

If the birthday child comes to their house, they always celebrate with a party dinner and a chocolate cinnamon sheet cake–the same cake Mary's mother made for her kids' birthdays. This should keep Mary very busy cooking, as she has eight grandchildren!

"Nan" Georgan gives her grandchildren "lessons" of some kind–dance, gymnastics, piano, etc., or she treats them to a special event like a live performance of *Lion King* or Holiday on Ice. Programs and photos of the children at these events, along with the memories they evoke, can be saved for their scrapbooks.

"Gramma" Bev from Wyoming tries to be with her grandchildren on their birthdays if possible; although they live in Alaska, Alabama, and Missouri, as well as southern Wyoming. The twin granddaughters who live in Independence, Missouri, asked one grandmother to plan a tea party for them and their friends and the other grandmother to take them bowling! The girls helped plan the parties, taking into account the varied interests of the grandmothers.

Bev and husband Jack also gave a very unusual gift to granddaughter, Samantha, who lived in the basement or lower level of her house in Cheyenne, Wyoming.

The most unusual birthday gift for a grandchild was when "Grump" and "Gramma" built a "window well" garden in granddaughter Samantha's lower level bedroom window. I had always thought that the view of the 3-foot high metal window well was pretty dismal as the only view from Samantha's room.

We had so much fun designing and building a beautiful miniature garden in that space. We painted the walls of the well a soft sunny yellow. We then added some gravel for drainage at the bottom, then some fertile soil and planted a variety of flowering and green plants. The primrose proved to be especially successful, as they continued to bloom for several years.

Then we added some little artificial birds, bird houses, frogs, lady bugs and butterflies. Finally, we added a clear plastic top with a grow-light attached, although the natural light that came in was probably sufficient.

Gramma Bev and Jack had so much fun doing it, and I'm sure that Samantha was reminded daily of their deep love for her.

As you can see, you don't have to give a "thing" as a birthday gift–it might be a trip of special interest to the child. Mary Ostlund relates, "The most unusual gift we ever gave any of our grandchildren was to Chad on his 15th birthday. John, a graduate of the Naval Academy, and I were invited to San Diego to sail on the *U. S. S. Cheyenne*, a nuclear submarine, on and under the Pacific Ocean. We received permission for Chad to be with us and he had a wonderful day. His classmates could not believe that he had been on the sub, AND under the sea!"

Grandmother "Dinah" Coffey found it difficult to find something for granddaughter Claire, whose birthday is in January–too soon after Christmas! Since she has never flown before, Diane and Claire's mother flew with her to Dallas on her birthday. They went ice skating and had lunch with friends–a "perfect" day, according to Claire.

Another favorite "Dinah" gift for all of her grandchildren is the blanket she crochets for each one when he/she is born. When they are six or seven years old, she makes bigger ones in their favorite colors. They always bring them when they spend the night, and she repairs them as needed.

Dinah has 13 grandchildren, so there are 13 birthdays to celebrate! The tradition is to have a family birthday party for each of them. *Everyone* comes–all four moms and dads, all the cousins–even though they live in different cities! They pray especially for the birthday child and give thanksgiving for him/her. "The kids love it!"

Our own grandchildren are very small (6, 4, and 18 months as of this writing), and seem to enjoy whatever we give them, OR they are being polite in not telling us if they don't! We enjoy giving gifts at unexpected times. At birthday parties they seem so overwhelmed with ALL the gifts, it doesn't appear that they have time to enjoy them! As soon as the child shows an interest in one toy, he is encouraged to stop playing and open the next. The pile of wrapping paper makes one worry that something might be thrown away–*and* not even be missed!

As we find something that we think they might enjoy, we put it in a drawer and wait for an opportunity to give it to them. (I must admit, however, that we usually don't wait too long!) It is a challenge to find age-appropriate toys, since we are "out of the loop" when it comes to the child's world! For that reason, I have included in Appendix B some ideas and resources for favorite toys for various age groups. Of course, the parents are also a great resource, since they keep up with what's "hot".

I think, as grandparents, our role is a little different from the parents. Perhaps we have the perspective to see what the child might "need" rather than "want". Perhaps the child just needs "time"–time in the garden, time at the zoo, time to learn a skill, time to walk, time to sled after a new snow, time to talk, time to listen to Grandma's stories about when she was a little girl. This precious commodity is perhaps too rare in the homes of these working moms. Grandparents also have time to read the newspaper and are aware of things to do in the community–concerts in the park, special library programs, museum exhibits for children, special events for children.

Chapter Eight

TRAVELS WITH GRANDMA

don't personally remember traveling with my grandma. My grandparents didn't drive, nor did they have the money for trips. I didn't drive until after I was married, and then we lived overseas, so I never had an opportunity to take her anywhere either. I do, however, look forward to many adventures with our grandchildren and hope to "follow in the footsteps" of these very creative travel-planning grandmas!

Many grandmas I know plan annual family vacations–a time when all of their children and grandchildren, who are often spread out across the nation, can be together. This allows the children to get to know their aunts, uncles, and cousins. They look forward to these times together–just hanging out! This is not an easy task, because it is difficult to get away from work and responsibilities, BUT after they do it once or twice, the children MAKE time for these vacations. It needn't be at an expensive resort–it can be a camping trip to a state park, a fishing trip, a fun trip to the Branson area, to a church camp, or to a beach.

The "author" of these family trips for us was Mary Anne Price, who has taken her six daughters and their families on family vacations twice each year since the first grandchild was born. One of these annual trips is to "The River" in south Texas, where they reserve eight of the 60 rooms. It is not fancy, and they just enjoy playing cards, swimming, playing tennis, or just talking, relaxing, and playing games. They have also vacationed as a family in Colorado, Florida, Kansas, and Arkansas.

One winter when they went skiing in Colorado, we were fortunate to be invited to share their family vacation. Mary Anne has had much practice cooking for "the masses", so I was intrigued with her art of simplifying and yet providing wonderful nutritious and delicious meals. One breakfast specialty included placing a piece of bacon around the inside of a muffin cup; then breaking an egg into the center and baking. Easy and delicious!

To keep Grandma from being overworked, families could sign up for meals and KP. To make it more fun, you could place everyone's name in a hat and draw names for duties. This would allow members of different families to "work" together.

We have observed over the years how close the cousins have become, growing up together in this way. They have a real sense of the importance of the family and look forward to their time together. When difficult times occur, they are there for each other.

Another grandma friend, Diane Coffey, and her entire family take trips to the beach near Ft. Walton, Florida. Every year they go to Navarre Beach for a week. "Every age loves the beach!"   They rent five rooms, and the grandchildren stay in different rooms with cousins, aunts, and uncles. Braden, who is 5, said very authoritatively to the younger ones, "Cousins are just like brothers and sisters. They just live in different houses."   The grandchildren range in age from 3 to 17, and Diane says "It's so fun to see Alexander, who is 15, tossing the football with his 5-year-old cousins." She thinks that building relationships with cousins is a huge benefit of these family trips.

Since there are too many of them to go out to eat, they have established alternative dining traditions. "Dinah" is in charge of breakfast. Lunch is simple– most everyone can make his own sandwich. The four families take turns preparing dinner for everyone. One night they order pizza. They don't go anywhere–they just enjoy being on the beach–the guys play golf, and the girls have outlet malls nearby. They *do* go to church together! The Fellowship Bible Church welcomes the entire family every year.

Certainly, a favorite destination for young children *is* the beach!! Just watching the waves roll in, building castles in the sand, collecting shells, digging for crabs, playing in the water happily occupy their time! There is probably a lesson here–no need for fancy toys or amusement parks! They are just happy "hanging out" with family. Favorite seaside vacation spots are the white-sand beaches of Destin, Sandestin, Seaside, Seagrove, Fort Walton Beach in Florida, and the San Diego area in California. Some families choose to go there year after year rather than opting for a different vacation spot each year. Their family "history" is there!

Mom Betty has made many family trips with her grandchildren and their parents–to Destin and Disneyworld in Florida; Silver Dollar City, near Branson, Missouri; and various locations in Colorado. She said that you must have "ground rules"; for example, each child gets to choose one thing he/she would like to do–no complaining when it's someone else's turn to choose!" On trips to Colorado, they just enjoy playing games–cards, board games, etc. Of course, that includes lots of popcorn and M & M's! She thinks that trips with the grandchildren alone are great, too! They've taken them fishing at Gaston's resort and Shangrila Resort near Grove, Oklahoma.

"G'ma" Anita Ibison said that that their favorite trip was to Beaver's Bend in southeastern Oklahoma. Each family had their own cabin, but the kids spent their time playing in G'ma's cabin, and different ones got to spend the night with her each night. She has found that they love these family trips because of the *availability* of their grandparents.

One of my favorite Grandma trip stories came from Grandmother Carol Headrick, who, with Grandfather Charles, has taken her grandchildren to the Lodge at Cloudcroft, New Mexico, for several years. The Lodge is supposed to be haunted, so the setting is perfect for Carol's love for storytelling and drama! (Carol is a renowned book reviewer throughout the state of Oklahoma.)

In addition to the ghost stories they share in the evening, the children enjoy hiking in the mountains, learning about the state they are in (the state bird, flower, etc.), swimming, going to museums, and the very popular "dressing up for dinner". They role-play proper etiquette and manners before they go to dinner–a wonderful learning experience!! They then practice their manners at dinner–probably to the amazement and admiration of all of the others in the dining room!!

At the beginning of the driving trip, they all change names. It might be a name their parents *thought* of naming them, or it can be purely imaginary. There is only one rule–and all must abide by it. "You must not interrupt, criticize, put down or correct anyone." This prevents their saying "DUH!" which Carol abhors! She interviews all of the children in the car–asking them about dreams, goals, and emotions. She uses the time to point out strengths and talents of each child. She encourages them to talk about feelings–"What made you the maddest? saddest? happiest?" Carol, who was a professor in the speech pathology department at OSU, teaches them sign language and takes advantage of any opportunity for learning.

Carol gives each child a disposable camera at the beginning of the trip, so he/she can record all of their adventures. After the trip, Carol makes a scrapbook for each one, using photos and adding a narrative of the trip. The children treasure these, and no doubt, they will show them someday to their own children and grandchildren! I wonder where *they* will take their grandchildren!

Joshua Carpenter, age 6, challenged his grandma one day, "Momo, let's take a trip!" to which she replied, "We might climb Mt. Everest." They went to Chicago instead to see Michael Jordan. OSU basketball coach Eddie Sutton got them tickets! They were there three days. They stayed on the pier and went to museums, the ball game, and Michael Jordan's restaurant, but one of his favorite activities was going up and down on the escalators, which are not available in Stillwater, Oklahoma, where they live.

When Sara Carpenter was 6, Momo took her to San Diego because she wanted to go to the ocean. They saw Sea World, the San Diego Zoo, and Balboa Park. Such fun!! They planned the trip together. They took lots of pictures and together they made a 3-page section to add to the scrapbook Sara's mom had already in progress. Rachael, age 6, will have her turn this year!!

Some grandmothers are fortunate to have a vacation house or cabin. "Gramouse" Dona Cooper is one such grandmother, who takes full advantage of this opportunity. She and "Doc" go to the family cabin near Cuchara, Colorado, where the grandchildren have "grown up". Like many, her children are scattered, so this is an opportunity to get everyone together. They stay there in the summer months, so all four families can plan a vacation trip at a time that is most convenient for them. Life is simple there—hiking, picking wildflowers, studying rocks, making cookies ("millions of them!"), playing games, making popcorn, sitting in front of the fire and sharing stories. Gramouse Dona is encouraged to read her poems, many of which focus on their family times at the cabin. A favorite is

SEVEN WONDERS OF OUR WORLD

The seven wonders of our world
(In '87 as the flag unfurled)
Were all together on the 4th of July
In Cuchara Valley, where mountain meets sky –
These merry makers of holiday noise –
Four giggling girls–three boisterous boys,
Celebrated from dawn until dark
By hiking, fishing, a fair in the park,
Overnight campout, a horseback ride
With weathered Earl again, as the guide.
They brightened the meadow, these colorful cousins
And ate Gramouse's cookies, some by the dozens.
They fed the chipmunks, spotted deer,
Watched the bluebirds, who built this year
A nest near the window, so all could see
A show more exciting than any TV.
They read all the books sent out by Uncle Tad;
 Played ping-pong, card games (until one would get mad).
 They made the parade more than a blink of the eye
As rock stars, Sheena, and a cutie pie,
Ballerina Beauties, a fisherman, too,
And when all the camera clicking was through,
They went to LaVeta's rodeo
With their Granddad-Doc and what a show!

They laughed with the clowns; drank lots of Coke,
Watched broncos buck off the brave cowpokes.
They roasted wieners–marshmallows, charred,
And as campfire singers, each one of them starred
In a rendition (with a clapping band)
Of "He's Got the Whole World in His Hands".
Which included their loved ones, who are very
 Wonderful parents–Kevin and Cheri,
Cathy and Roge, Peggy and Chip,
Who shared with them the joys of this trip.
Since these seven wonders of our world
So quickly past our lives are whirled,
We grasp for posterity with the pen
These treasured moments to recall again
Of grandchildren, ages 8 to 3
Named Cadee, Jesse, and Karson Lee,
Kannon, Andee, Kolby and Nat
Who have convinced their grandparents that
They have each one been heaven-sent
To fill our lives with wonderment.

As the children get a little older, Disneyworld is a great place to be! In fact, you may send for a Disneyworld video produced especially for grandparents to help inspire and plan your trip. The Disney planners make sure your trip is hassle-free! The various theme parks within Disneyworld offer lots of variety, and the accommodations are perfect for everyone! We have gone twice and have marveled at how Disney has "bridged the generation gap"! *Everyone* loves Disneyworld! I would encourage you to stay at a Disneyworld property.

Each property or hotel has appeal for different interests, gender, and age groups.

As grandchildren enter their teens, it becomes more difficult to find things that they can enjoy with grandparents. Skiing is one they enjoy if you're up to it! Many ski resorts cater to families–Breckenridge, Keystone, and Copper Mountain near Denver, Colorado; Steamboat in northern Colorado, and Durango in the south. Many have ski schools and instructors who give lessons to children and teens. Smaller ski areas, such as Terry Peak in the Black Hills of South Dakota, or Taos in New Mexico are wonderful for novices. They have snow tubing and snowmobiling as well. "Honna" Judy Morrison loves their family ski trips at Whistler in Canada. They enjoy playing in the snow with Wyatt and Cooper (ages 5 and 2), going on sleigh rides, baking, and snuggling by the fire.

Some grandmas have "Cousin Camps", where all the grandchildren come at one time to enjoy one another. These usually require more structure and daily "lesson plans" and are easier when you live in a place which has lots to do within walking distance. An example would be Gramma Bev, who lives with "Grump" Jack in the Grand Tetons National Park in Wyoming. They step out on their deck and have a magnificent view of the Tetons. They can hike, watch for wildlife, visit the beavers making a lodge in a nearby stream, watch the swans nest at Pacific Creek, and go on picnics. "Grump" Jack can teach them the basics of water color painting, and they can try their hand at painting one of the beautiful landscapes to take home.

They can all pile in a van and go on to spectacular Yellowstone National Park, stopping on the way for short hikes or excursions and looking at special places of interest never seen before. They can add a trip to Jenny Lake or String Lake for a special birthday picnic, swimming or hiking. They are making memories these cousins will never forget!! and what fun to do them together!!

Another great idea for a "cousins' camp" came from the "Family Network" section of *Better Homes and Gardens* (December, 2001). The writer from West Palm Beach, Florida, shared; "A friend of mine hosts weeklong 'camps' at her home for six of her great-grandchildren. This year's theme was Native American culture, and the activities included crafts, sewing, cooking, and even cleaning. The children created masks, drums, rattles, and dream catchers. They designed replicas of a tribal council house. All of them kept daily journals of their experiences. She structured the days so that no one had a chance to get bored."

Grandma Mary and husband John are rarely able to take trips with their grandchildren, but they, too, entertain them at their home–Remount Ranch, a wonderful setting between Cheyenne and Laramie, Wyoming. The grandchildren make trips from their homes to visit Mary and John and often spend holidays and vacations with them.

Mary reminisces, "They all learned to ride and care for horses, became very proficient at finding and observing wildlife, and learned to appreciate the magnificent Wyoming night sky by spending nights outside in bed rolls. My hobby is bird watching, and we spend many hours together searching for and finding these feathered creatures. The intensity of weather– the snowstorms, thunderstorms, sunrises, and sunsets always fascinate them."

When grandson Jordan was 12 years old, he spent a week at Remount, and below are excerpts from a school paper he wrote, describing his experiences:

"Tall pine trees swaying in the wind. Waves from the small lake washing up on the shore, birds chirping. Some of the things I like to do there are fishing in the lake and riding horses. The reason I like riding horses so much is because if I want to get away for a while, I can just saddle up and go for a long ride into the forest. I like to explore, and I usually see some deer. After supper we usually go on a porcupine hunt. The reason we hunt the porcupines is because they strip all the bark off the trees, which will kill them. One thing about my grandma is that she loves wildlife, especially birds and deer. If you ever shot a bird or a deer, she would shoot you!"

One unique travel idea is to take your grandchildren on a four-day cruise on the Mississippi River! You can start in New Orleans, which now abounds with child-friendly sights; then board the *American Queen* or one of the other Delta Queen steamboats, and enjoy a leisurely trip up the Mississippi. You can stop at the plantations along the route, enjoy the Cajun culture at the Rural Life Museum in Baton Rouge, OR you can simply stay on the ship to relish all of the activities it offers. After a hearty breakfast, you can play cards in the Mark Twain Lounge or just enjoy watching the river towns go by.

You must save room after lunch to enjoy the afternoon ice-cream bar and sit in the rockers on the deck, or enjoy afternoon tea in the parlor. After a five-course dinner in the evening, you can enjoy fabulous entertainment, geared to young people for this special child-friendly cruise. Since the state rooms accommodate only two people, the grandchildren can have a room of their very own—very liberating!! We have taken this river cruise, and Grandmother Carol and Charles Headrick have made this trip with their grandchildren. A great experience!

Additional great ideas for traveling with grandchildren are available from AARP. The following ideas from AARP were printed in Charlotte Lankard's column in *The Daily Oklahoman*, May 26, 2003:

1. Talk to the parents and the grandkids and find out what interests them. History? Science? Sports? Being outdoors? Do some early research. Gather ideas, and then let the children help choose. For younger kids, it might be a trip to the zoo, aquarium or museum. Older children may enjoy an adventure away from home.

2. Try a state or national park. If you're up for really grand adventures, watch Old Faithful geyser erupt at Yellowstone, raft in the Grand Canyon, hike the Appalachian Trail, explore

ancient American Indian dwellings at Mesa Verde or visit a Civil War battlefield.

3. A trip to the beach? A cruise? Or if you opt for a city trip, older children might enjoy the theater, a sports event, or an art museum.

4. Explore the idea of a volunteer vacation with older grandchildren. The American Hiking Society offers volunteer trips on which hikers conduct trail maintenance part of the day and spend the rest of the day hiking and enjoying the outdoors.

5. Elderhostel (www.elderhostel.org) will send you a catalog of a complete list of grandparent/grandchild trips–worldwide educational adventures.

6. Consider how long the trip should be. If a traveler is younger than six, probably a day trip or maybe one overnight is best. Elementary-age children can handle a week. High schoolers might last two weeks, as long as you plan together things you'll both enjoy doing.

7. Know their daily routines, nap times, safety needs, medicines, bed times, allergies, and food preferences. Set up rules in case the child gets lost or separated from you. Inexpensive two-way radios? Walkie-Talkies? Cell phones?

8. Remember that kids need to burn off more energy during the day than you do, so take time out for them to play–a swim in the hotel pool or a couple of hours at a nearby playground.

9. Take small games, books, music, toys and art supplies. In case of rain or long waits at restaurants or airports, you'll have things to keep them busy.

10. Take snacks. Yogurt and granola bars are preferable to sugary or high-fat foods. Be sure they drink a lot of water or juice to stay hydrated. And, of course, an occasional candy bar, soft drink or ice cream should not be overlooked.

11. Be flexible! Don't have every minute planned. Leave room for spontaneous adventures.

12. Most of all, have fun and be open-minded and enthusiastic. And on the way home, talk about where you will want to go next year!

It should be noted, however, that you don't have to travel to distant places to have a good time with your grandchildren!! You can take them to a hotel nearby–preferably one with an indoor pool. You can swim, play cards or games in the lobby area, enjoy a special video in the room, complete with snacks and drinks, enjoy dinner at a child-friendly restaurant, and, if you've selected the hotel carefully, you can enjoy a breakfast buffet right there! No clean-up afterward, no dishes to wash! "What a deal!" reports Grandmother "Suzy" Timberlake, who enjoys the Embassy Suites in Dallas! We like the Renaissance Hotel in Tulsa.

Chapter Nine

FINDING GOD WITH GRANDMA

ne of the greatest privileges for grandmas is to help their grandchildren develop a relationship with their creator. This is the greatest gift she can give them!! There are many ways "Grandma" can share her faith and help her grandchildren begin their faith journey.

Pray for your grandchildren before they are born! Pray each day that this little baby will be healthy physically, mentally, emotionally, and *spiritually!* With today's technology we get to know them before they are born! We get to watch them move on the ultrasound; we can know the sex of the baby; we can give him or her a name! We can pray specifically for this precious creation–for their healthy development of body *and* spirit.

Once they arrive, pray with them. Kneel beside their beds with them and listen to their prayers *or* teach them to pray if needed. Don't assume they are too young! A friend told me the other day that her 3-year-old granddaughter insisted that she kneel with her to pray and recited from memory the entire "Lord's Prayer"!! Pray at meals when they come to visit. Teach them to pray for guidance in every area of their lives.

I remember daily devotions led by my Aunt Lucy, who became "Grandma" to our girls when my mother died. My daughters still remember her as a spiritual role model.

Pray for their choice of mates. Let them know you are praying. When they are older, make a list together of the qualities they want in a mate. Encourage them to pray for that special one and to look for the one with those qualities. This may help them be more objective when the "love bug bites"!

Let them see you as someone who puts her faith into action. "Gramouse" Dona believes that we speak through our actions–things we do and say around home. When we visited them at their cabin in Colorado, we saw first hand an example of this. Grandchildren were present to witness their early morning ritual. After breakfast, Doc would say to Dona, "This is the day the Lord has made." Dona replied, "Let us rejoice and be glad in it." Then together they said, "And may we be a blessing to someone today."

In their home a picture of Christ hangs over their kitchen table. Also on their kitchen walls are scriptures written in calligraphy. Gramouse believes you should *show* the importance of the Bible and the place God has in your lives. She says, "The way you live your lives is the best lesson! Children seem to respond better to that than words."

Dona's name "Gramouse" reflects this same lesson of commitment to one's faith. For 26 years she wrote a column for her church's newsletter called "Tidbits by the Church Mouse"–"praise things" of interest to the congregation. In her home office she has a collection of mice, and when granddaughter Cadee started talking, she called her "Gramouse", and it caught on. Dona and Grand-Doc have also taught Sunday School for 22 years. Her grandchildren are able to see her faith through this long-term commitment. She says, "It is my prayer that the grandchildren will put their faith in God and make a commitment to serve Him."

Another grandma who leads by example is Gramma Bev. "We always attend church with our grandchildren when we visit them and take them to our church and Sunday School when they visit us. We try to pray with them regularly–at meal times, and especially to share in bedtime prayers. We also encourage them to go to God in prayer when they are frustrated, angry, worried or frightened." Bev was a surrogate grandmother to our children when we lived in Wyoming. Going to church together, she was certainly one of their early Christian mentors.

Living in the shadow of the Tetons, Bev would agree with Grandma Mary who shares, "I think the ranch experience for our grandchildren helped them find God. I know it reinforced my belief. One cannot look at the beauty of the wilderness without believing that it and the creatures in it were created by God. The grandchildren were exposed to these wonders when they were very young and their minds very open."

Other Godly grandmothers have shared their faith with their grandchildren–

Mom Betty gives them at least one gift at Christmas which has religious significance–a book, a picture of Christ, a tiny cross, a framed scripture. Bible storybooks, audio tapes and video tapes are also good choices. She also gives them a prayer journal when they get older.

Nan Georgan talks with them and sings with them about Jesus. "They sometimes ask when I will die. That is a perfect chance for me to speak about my joy and happiness in my journey to Heaven."

Momo Suzanne sings songs with her grandchildren, accompanied by her ukulele. Their "special" Luke loves music and the repetition and will sit still and listen to Momo play her ukulele. He gives the sign for "more". She sings "Jesus Loves Me", interjecting Luke's name, "Jesus Loves Luke".

Grandmother Carol, a popular book reviewer, was able to share the "real Easter story" with her granddaughter, Emily, through the words of a beautiful letter written to her. I include the entire letter here because, as you will see, Carol shares more than the "real Easter story"–she shares her faith and love through the kind words of this very special letter.

Dear Emily,

I am at home all this week with your granddad because OSU is having Spring Break and all the students went home or on a trip so I am enjoying a vacation from school, too. Saturday and Sunday I sat at my desk in my little room upstairs writing a new review of a book that I will learn this week so I can tell it to groups of ladies who like to have lunch together and hear a story.

This new book is Farewell, I'm bound to Leave You by Fred Chappell. It is a story about a grandchild and a mother and a grandmother. It's a little sad because the grandmother is dying, but most of the story is happy and even funny because the grandchild and the mother are remembering all the fun things they did with the grandmother and especially they are remembering all the stories she told them.

Today a letter from your mother came in the mail, and I loved hearing all the things she wrote about you and Rebecca. I was so glad to hear how much you like playing with the Pick and Shop Marketplace that we sent you. I told your mother that before I wrapped it to mail, I got all the little pieces out and almost wanted to keep it to play with myself. Your mother also wrote that you are sharing the new bandanas with Rebecca, as I knew you would, and that you are ready to put your friends' names, addresses and phone numbers in the little address book we sent to you.

Your granddad and I are always so happy to hear that you like the things we send to you. This little package has some things we hope you and Rebecca will like reading and playing with during this Easter season. Your mother also told me that you are very interested in hearing about the real Easter story probably because you are old enough now to want to know true stories. The real Easter story is true because it is in the Bible , and you probably have heard it at your church.

The Easter story is really happy and sad like a lot of other good and true stories. I know you remember the Christmas story from the Bible about God's son, Jesus, being born to Mary and Joseph. Mary was just a young and plain girl who God knew would be a good mother to his son Jesus. Joseph was a little older and just a good plain man who was good at building things out of wood. God knew he would be a good husband to Mary and a good dad to Jesus while he lived on earth–before he went back to Heaven to live with his real father, God.

Remember, God made our whole world and everything in it, but he had never lived down here like us as a plain man. So maybe He thought it would be a good idea to let His only son Jesus come down here and live with plain people like us for a little while. Instead of sending him from Heaven to earth as a grown man or as a rich strong king (which God certainly could have done if he had wanted to), He thought the best idea would be to let Jesus be born as a new baby to Mary and grow up as a little kid in Mary and Joseph's home just like all the other little kids. Isn't it interesting that God didn't think that the best mother and dad He chose for Jesus to live with during his visit on earth had to be a rich king and queen or have the nicest house or even be the most popular? They were just plain and really good people.

Now Mary and Joseph understood from the beginning that this was really God's only son, and they were to be his parents only while he lived on earth. The Bible doesn't tell us much about his life as a little child except we know Mary and Joseph were really good parents to him because the Bible tells us that he grew in four very important ways: (Luke 2:52)

1.   **Intellectually**–He listened to good stories and read and studied so he would learn a lot and use his mind and memory so he could teach.

2.   **Physically**–He grew strong by exercising and eating and sleeping right so he would be healthy.

3. **Spiritually**–He read the books of the Old Testament in the Bible, (The New Testament hadn't been written then.) and he prayed to God, his father in heaven, probably a lot every day and night.

4. **Socially**–He was kind and fair and honest and friendly to others, so that he would have friends who liked to be with him.

We do know when Jesus was 12, he was really interested in hearing his parents and preachers and other men who studied the Bible tell Bible stories to him. Then when he was old enough to leave home, he left and took some of his good friends and began to teach all the people who would listen about his father, God. Many of the people who heard him talk and tell stories liked him and believed everything he said and wanted to hear more. I'm sure you know about many of the stories he told and the things he did for his friends and children and adults. He traveled by walking and in boats with his friends teaching people who would listen until he was about 33 years old.

Some of the people who listened to him did not believe that he could be God's son, so they said he was lying. Some of the leaders and kings were jealous of him and were afraid he might become more important and popular than they were. So some of these people got together to think of a way they could get rid of Jesus and they decided to kill him.

Jesus knew what these people were saying and planning, and, of course, God knew because He knows everything. We know that Jesus or God could have stopped these men from doing these terrible things like whipping and killing him, but they didn't. I think God wanted us to know how much he loved us by letting his only son come to earth and live with plain people like us. Then God showed that He loved us even more than our mothers and dads love us by letting Jesus be killed. I think this made God as sad as it would make any dad to see his child be hurt or killed, but He knew He could make Jesus come back to life.

Jesus was killed on the cross on Friday, and they buried him just like they did others who died. But early on Sunday morning (which we now call Easter Sunday), when Jesus' friends went to his grave and were still so sad because he was dead, the grave was open, and he was gone. He was alive again, and God let him stay on earth a few more days to see his friends and talk with them, so they would understand that he was alive and so they wouldn't be sad anymore. Then he went up into Heaven to live with God, and I think they were probably so happy to be back together. Jesus told his friends he was going to make a place for them and all of us who believe in God and him can come someday and live with them in Heaven, too.

So although that Friday was so scary and sad, Easter Sunday was the happiest day for everyone. Every Easter since has been happy because we remember how much God loved us, and we know that Jesus came back to life on Easter and now is alive in Heaven with God.

Emily, you know the way you get to really know someone is to talk with them and listen to them. And if they live far away like we do, you can also get to know them better by reading the letters they write to you or by talking on the phone. Well, the way you can know God and Jesus better is by talking and listening to them by praying and listening to stories about them at home and at church, and reading the

Bible when you learn to read. I think the best thing about having Jesus as a friend to talk to when we pray is that we know he will understand every feeling we have because he lived here and had all the same feelings like being sad, happy, lonely, hurt, scared, excited and even mad. So no matter how we feel, we can talk to him about it because he will understand.

Happy Easter!
I love you,

Grandmother
March 10, 1997

What a beautiful testimony of faith AND love for one's grandchild!

I know many grandchildren who are blessed with Godly parents, who take them to church and Sunday School and pray in their homes. We need to support them in their efforts to teach their children the lessons of faith. Grandma Lois Brewster, who has twelve grandchildren born to only two children, says "I hope the prayers my grandchildren and I have said together and the talks we sometimes have had will reinforce the teachings their parents are providing."

Grams Mary Anne Price includes a Bible verse on cards and letters sent to her grandchildren. She hopes that, as they look up these verses, they will develop a habit of looking for answers to their problems in the Bible.

When grandmother "Dinah" is on her chaise lounge, the grandchildren know that she is there for her Bible study or prayer. Children certainly do what we do—rather than what we say, don't they?! She hopes that her grandchildren are learning devotion to God and unselfishness. She thinks that selfishness is the most pervasive of all sins.

When a grandchild is baptized, "Dinah" gives him/her a Bible and writes each one a letter. In the letter she shares her personal testimony, gives them advice, and tells them about the gift of the Holy Spirit, which will be their "Abiding Comforter" throughout their lives. To a teenager who seems to be faced daily with decisions and crises, this is a wonderful promise and source of strength.

Grammar Pat Downs says, "There is nothing we can do with our grandchildren that is more important than to help them find God and His love and to develop a personal relationship with Him. This is our daily prayer for them."

"It is so important to read the Bible with these little ones. I try to read the scriptures with them every chance I get—regardless of how tired I am!" Pat believes in the command given in Deuteronomy 11:18-19:

> Fix these words of mine in your hearts and minds; tie them as symbols on your hands and bind them on your foreheads. Teach them to your children, talking about them when you sit at home and when you walk along the road, when you lie down and when you get up.

In 1993 Pat and her husband wrote *Turning Minutes Into Memories: Our Story.* The paperback book begins with Psalm 139 and the following statement: "Often our prayers include the yet unborn grandchildren, so with the prospect of that, we have decided to share personal memories of our early childhood and faith as a legacy for another generation." Jack, who is 8, just recently discovered and read his copy and laughed at how many times "Pops" mentioned snakes!

Living by example, telling or reading Bible stories to our grandchildren, or watching Bible videotapes with them; praying with them, listening to their sweet prayers, singing songs with them, going caroling at Christmas, taking them to church, encouraging them to depend upon Him and ask for His help, praying for them, praying for their spouses, taking time to listen to their questions about God and their faith journey– are all ways grandmothers can help them develop a personal relationship with their Creator, God, and help them to know of His love for them. They can't have a relationship with someone they don't know! All of these activities will help them become acquainted with Him and become aware of His great power and love for them.

Chapter Ten

LONG DISTANCE GRANDMAS!

$\mathcal{M}$any of us do not have the good fortune of living near our grandchildren. My heart aches for my dear friend, Judy, in Edmond, Oklahoma, who must commute to Seattle, Washington, to see her two precious grandbabies!! However, she and several other very clever friends have found ways to stay connected!

Honna Judy buys an age-appropriate book and tapes herself reading it. She can tape a greeting at the beginning. She then mails it to her little Wyatt and Cooper, and they LOVE it!! They play it over and over. Tapes of such sweet messages to the grandchildren are very popular and help them to keep in touch!! Taping a *Little Bear* book, sending the book and a little bear to sleep with is another variation; or taping a book about trucks and send a truck, another idea. Radio Shack has some technology and Pottery Barn had a bear a few years ago that would allow for a personal message to be recorded in it. Even a talking birthday card is special—they love to hear your voice!

Grandmas can send gifts for special occasions or *anytime* you want to show your love. The "thought" is certainly the key here, but doing the tiniest bit of research will make the gift especially meaningful!! What is age-appropriate? What is "in" with that age group now? Mom and Dad or your other Grandma friends can help you here! We may not know who Dora or Builder Bob or Blues Clues is, but we can find help in making our selections!! (See Appendix A and Appendix B for resources for toys, games, and books.)

Although in an ideal world, it would be best to deliver the gift in person, the children love to get packages in the mail!! And Mom and Dad can help them to see how much you love them—to go to all that work to wrap and send it! After all, the object is to let them feel your love!!

Other ideas for keeping in touch include

1. Make regular phone calls. Set up a time each week to call, and when you call, ask for the grandchild. "Grams" Mary Anne has an 800 number, so they can call her anytime. And they do!

2. Send funny cards with stickers or sticks of gum inside

3. Send recent photos of grandma and grandpa—of your activities, travel, etc. Send postcards from places you travel.

4. Encourage the parents to use a fax machine or scanner to send some of the grandchildren's just-completed art work.

5. Write notes or letters or e-mails! Parents can let you know what is going on in their lives, so you can write about these things. As children get older, they can correspond themselves.

6. Write poems for your grandchild, celebrating special occasions when you cannot be present.

7. Travel to be with them, if possible. These visits are very special because they *don't* see you very often, and many times these trips are to celebrate special occasions in their lives.

8. When you visit, try visiting your grand-children's schools, attending their activities, and meeting their friends.

Gramouse Dona Cooper wrote this poem after she visited granddaughter Kellee's class on Grandparents' Day:

SOME GRANDPARENTS ARE...

Some grandparents are short,
Some grandparents are tall.
Some have hair of gray;
Some have none at all.

Some have a few wrinkles.
Some have extra chins.
Some have extra bear hugs.
Some have extra grins.
Some wear bifocals.
Some wear business suits.
Some wear hearing aids.
Some wear cowboy boots.

Some live down the street.
Some in another state.
Some help you mind your manners.
Some let you stay up late.

But though grandparents may be different
In age and shape and size,
One thing that makes them all alike–
And this comes as no surprise,
Is that *their* grandchildren in Mrs. Glover's room
Are just the best in every way
And so each morning for them becomes
Another happy GRANDPARENT'S DAY!!!

9. If the parents own a digital camera, they can download pictures immediately following a special event and send to the grandparents attached to an e-mail describing the event.

10. Volunteer to keep the grandchildren when the parents must be gone. What a great opportunity to have them all to yourself!! But, as Gramma Bev points out–if you are going to keep the grand- children, it is important, though difficult, to *discipline* them. As with their parents, children see discipline as an expression of love and a source of security.

Grandparents Who Are Deceased

Grandchildren should be encouraged to "know their grandparents"–to have some connection or memory– even if they are deceased.   My mother died suddenly when my daughters were 5 and 2 ½.   She was such a remarkable woman that I was especially saddened that they would not experience her influence in their lives. To help them know and remember her, I made a "memory box" (which was popular then), placing in it those things that represented her varied interests.

My mother was a gifted seamstress, so at the center was a picture of a woman sewing and in the other sections were a photo of her at church camp, a crossword puzzle with a tiny pencil, buttons spelling her name, "LOLA ACOSTA"; tiny books to represent her love for reading, a tiny Bible showing how important her faith was, and a photo of her with her grandchildren. Each section gave me the opportunity to share memories of her. Grandchildren need to know their history–the "stock" from whence they came.

This same result could be achieved through the pages of a scrapbook–even a photo album. Our youngest daughter, now grown, shared on a recent visit, "I think I really would have liked Grandma Lola." When I asked why she felt that way, she said that she had been looking at the photos in my mother's *old* photo album, which was lying on the bedside table. These concrete remembrances help reinforce the stories we tell them of their grandparents.

Chapter Eleven

What do You Wish You Had Done with Your Grandchildren??

$\mathcal{M}$ ost of us want to live our lives with few regrets. We don't want "would'a, could'a, should'a" times, but we all know that hindsight gives us a chance to share what we have learned with others. For this reason, I want to share some insights from dear grandma friends.

Although Nan Betty has kept a journal to record the funny things the grandchildren have said and done over the years, she wishes she had written a letter to her grandchildren on every birthday–telling about the last year's events and what she enjoyed doing with them; how they made her proud; what she thought they had learned. It's not too late! Great ideas!

Grams Mary Anne wished she had read more and listened more. Nan Georgan wishes that she had recorded more of their voices on tape–to have kept one on-going tape for each grandchild of their utterances from the very beginning. "Recording all their voice mail messages would have been a hoot and a joy!"

"My wish is still possible," relates Grandma Mary Ostlund who lives in Cheyenne, Wyoming. She would like to travel with the grandchildren, one or two at a time, to New York, where she grew up. They could go to a Broadway play, to a Yankee ballgame, see the Statue of Liberty and other tourist attractions. As a Catholic, she would love to take them to St. Patrick's Cathedral and visit St. Vincent Hospital, where she attended nursing school. "I don't think this is an 'ego' thing (and if you knew Mary, you wouldn't think that for a minute!). I just would like for them to experience the Big City that I grew up in and to learn about a completely different area of our country."

A regret that many grandmothers shared was that they were not able to spend more time with their grandchildren–especially those who lived far away. Most children have needs, and in an age where divorce is so prevalent, grandparents can fill a real void in their lives. My Grandma Mellie played such an important part in my life–providing a "safe and secure place" in the midst of a home life that was far from perfect. My most pleasant memories are those spent with her in Greenfield, Oklahoma!

I appreciate so much a comment made by Grandmother Carol: "We need to realize that there will be a time when our grandchildren won't want to be with us!! We need to take advantage of the few precious years we have with them." We sometimes get "too busy"–a regret we often express when talking about our own children. Let's not make that same mistake with our grandchildren!

Appendix A:

TOYS AND GAMES

Old doll–worn, torn and tattered.
You were my friend when it really mattered!
Anonymous

The selection of toys is important–not just in terms of safety, but in the light of what is appropriate for the grandchild's developmental stage and interests.

Age-Appropriate Toys

The following is a list of toys that the American Academy of Pediatrics recommends for specific age groups. It suggests that you use these recommendations when shopping for toys.

Newborn to 1-year-old baby

Choose brightly-colored, lightweight toys that appeal to your baby's sight, hearing and touch.

1. Cloth, plastic or board books with large pictures
2. Large blocks of wood or plastic

3. Pots and pans
4. Rattles
5. Soft, washable animals, dolls or balls
6. Bright mobiles that are out of baby's reach
7. Busy boards
8. Floating bath toys
9. Squeeze toys

1 to 2-year-old toddler

Toys for this age group should be safe and be able to withstand a toddler's curious nature.

1. Cloth, plastic or board books with large pictures
2. Sturdy dolls
3. Kiddy cars
4. Musical tops
5. Nesting blocks
6. Push and pull toys (no long strings)
7. Stacking toys
8. Toy telephones (without cords)

2-to 5-year-old preschooler

Toys for this age group can be creative or imitate the activity of parents and older children.

1. Books (short stories or action stories)
2. Blackboard and chalk

3. Building blocks
4. Crayons, nontoxic finger paints, clay
5. Hammer and bench
6. Housekeeping toys
7. Outdoor toys: sandbox (with a lid), slide, swing, playhouse
8. Transportation toys (tricycles, cars, wagons)
9. Tape or record player
10. Simple puzzles with large pieces
11. Dress-up clothes
12. Tea party utensils

5- to 9-year-old child

Toys for this age group should help your child develop new skills and creativity.

1. Blunt scissors, sewing sets
2. Card games
3. Doctor and nurse kits
4. Hand puppets
5. Balls
6. Bicycles with helmets
7. Crafts
8. Electric trains
9. Paper dolls
10. Jump ropes
11. Roller skates with protective gear
12. Sports equipment
13. Table games

10- to 14-year-old child

Hobbies and scientific activities are ideal for this age group.

1. Computer games
2. Sewing, knitting, needlework
3. Microscopes/telescopes
4. Table and board games
5. Sports equipment
6. Hobby collections

TOYS ON-LINE:

There are hundreds of web-sites for children's toys and games!! I've listed just a few that you may want to look at, but they have everything!!

Educational toys and games
Creative toys and games
Vintage toys
Pioneer toys
American Civil War toys
Christian toys and games
Indoor and outdoor games and toys
Wooden toys
Computer toys
Discovery games

Toy and game companies have web-sites:

> Toys "R" Us
> Fisher Price
> Mattel
> Hasbro
> Sears Toys
> Wal-mart Toys
> Target Toys, and
> Amazon has a web-site for toys and games

You can order toys and games from all over the world!

> UK toys
> German toys, and any country you might
> think of!

There are even web-sites for

> Hard-to-find toys
> Toys and games for every age and holiday season
> Party games and costumes

AND one for Grandkids Toys–Children's Toys, Books and Games!!

CHILDREN'S BOOKS

To capture our grandchildren's interest in reading, I think it is important to locate age-appropriate books and, of course, books that match their interests. A book that was very helpful to me in this regard was *Children's Literature in the Elementary School* by Charlotte S. Huck (Holt, Rinehart & Winston, New York, 1976, 3rd Edition, updated). In the chapter entitled, "Books for Ages and Stages", the author gives examples of books that are enjoyed by children of all ages.

PRESCHOOL AND KINDERGARTEN – Ages 3, 4, and 5

For rapid development of language –
Mother Goose
Mr. Gumpy's Outing, Burningham
Millions of Cats, Gag
Rosie's Walk, Hutchins
The Three Bears, Rockwell
Crash! Bang! Boom! Spier
Father Fox's Pennyrhymes, Watson
The Good Bird, Wezel
The Gingerbread Boy

Very active, short attention span

A B C, Burningham

The Cupboard, Burningham

Do *You Want to Be My Friend?* Carle

The Very Hungry Caterpillar, Carle

Pat the Bunny, Kunhardt

Puzzles, Wildsmith

**Interest, behavior and thinking
are egocentric—child-centered**

Grandfather and I, Buckley

The Snowy Day, Keats

Where Did My Mother Go? Preston

Noisy Nora, Wells

Curious about his world

Will I Have a Friend? Cohen

Best Friends for Frances, Hoban

Peter's Chair, Keats

My Doctor, Rockwell

**Builds concepts through
many first-hand experiences**

Anno's Counting Book, Anno

Big Ones, Little Ones, Hoban

Co*unt and See,* Hoban

Sar*a and the Door,* Jensen

The *Listening Walk, Showers*

Child has little sense of time. Time is "before now", "now", and "not yet".

Seasons, Burningham
The Grouchy Ladybug, Carle
It's Time Now, Tresselt
Over and Over, Zolotow

Child learns through imaginative play.

Mike Mulligan and His Steam Shovel, Burton
May I Bring a Friend? Deregniers
Just Me, Ets
Corduroy, Freeman
The Train, McPhail

Seeks warmth and security in relationships with adults

Goodnight, Moon, Brown
Amifika, Clifton
Ask Mr. Bear, Flack
Good-Night, Owl! Hutchins
Little Bear, Minarik
I Don't Care, Sharmat

Beginning to assert his independence. Takes delight in his accomplishments.

I Hate to Go to Bed, Barrett
The Runaway Bunny, Brown
The Carrot Seed, Krauss
Benjie, Lexau
The Temper Tantrum Book, Preston
Moving, Watson

**Beginning to make value judgments;
what is fair? what should be punished?**

Keep Running, Allen Bulla
Titch, Hutchins
The Little Engine that Could, Piper
The *Tale of Peter Rabbit,* Potter
The Tale of Benjamin Bunny, Potter

PRIMARY–Ages 6 and 7

**Continued development
and expansion of language.**

Squawk to the Moon, Little Goose Preston
Amos and Boris, Steig
A Thousand Lights and Fireflies, Tresselt
Poetry of Aileen Fisher,
    Kuskin, McCord, Stevenson, *et al*

Attention span increasing.

Walter, the Lazy Mouse Flack
Frog and Toad Together, Lobel
Amelia Bedelia, Parish

**Striving to accomplish skills
demanded by adults**

When Will I Read? Cohen
Impossible, Possum Conford
Petunia, Duvoisin
Nobody Listens to Andrew, Guilfoile
Leo the Late Bloomer, Kraus

Learning still based upon immediate perception and direct experiences.

Wild Mouse, Brady
Look Again! Hoban
The Amazing Dandelion, Selsam
Guinea Pigs, All about Them, Silverstein

Continued interest in the world around him—eager and curious.

Green Grass and White Milk, Aliki
Journey to the Moon, Fuchs
Behind the Wheel, Koren
Fish Is Fish, Lionni
Digging for Dinosaurs, Swinton

Vague concepts of time

A Weed Is a Flower, Aliki
The Bears on Hemlock Mountain, Dalgliesh
Clocks and More Clocks, Hutchins
Obadiah the Bold, Turkle

More able to separate fantasy from reality; greater imagination.

Sam, Bangs, and Moonshine Ness
Where the Wild Things Are, Sendak
Caps for Sale, Slobodkina
The Great Big Enormous Turnip, Tolstoy

**Beginning to develop empathy
and understanding for others.**

    Evan's Corner, Hill
    Stevie, Steptoe
    Anna's Silent World, Wolf
    Crow Boy, Yashima

**Has a growing sense of justice;
demands rules.**

    Dandelion, Freeman
    The Surprise Party, Hutchins
    Let's Be Enemies, Udry
    The Judge, Zemach

Humor is developing.

    The Stupids Have a Ball, Allard
    *Animals Should Definitely
       Not Wear Clothing,* Barrett
    Lazy Tommy Pumpkinhead, DuBois
    Just Like Everyone Else, Kuskin

Beginning sexual curiosity.

    *The Wonderful Story
       of How You Were Born,* Gruenberg
    "Where Did I Come From?" Mayle
    Where Do Babies Come From? Sheffield

Physical contour of the body is changing; permanent teeth appear.

Whistle for Willie, Keats
Our Morning in Maine, McCloskey
I Did It, Rockwell

Continues to seek independence from adults.

Tim to the Rescue, Ardizzone
Train Ride, Steptoe
Henry the Explorer, Taylor
Ira Sleeps Over, Waber

Continues to need warmth and security in adult relationships.

In My Mother's House, Clark
Hush, Jon, Gill
My Mother Is the Most Beautiful Woman in the World, Reyher
Sam, Scott
Mr. Rabbit and the Lovely Present, Zolotow

Ms. Huck's recommendations for "Books for Ages and Stages" continues for ages 8 through 12, but by this time children are attaining independence in their reading skills, so I have not included the reading list for those levels. You certainly may consult her book or others for age-appropriate books for those age groups. She points out that children at ages 8 or 9 may be completely absorbed in their reading, or they may still be having difficulty in learning to read. In the latter case, the grandmother can certainly encourage the children and continue to read with them.

Children's Books On-Line:

Just as with toys and games, there are hundreds of web-sites for children's books. Listed below are some of the most popular ones:

1. **Barnes & Noble, Jr.: Children's Books**– includes reviews and recommendations.

2. **Powell's Books: Kids' Books**–includes reviews and recommendations of children's books, including picture books, middle readers, and young adult titles.

3. **Amazon.com Books: Kids**–includes reviews, recommendations and gift ideas.

4. **Scholastic, Inc**–publisher of children's books and supplementary learning aides for K-8. My personal favorite!! 1000's of inexpensive quality paperback books for children!

5. **Choose the Right Books for Kids**–includes lists of children's award-winning books and gives recommendations by age group.

6. **Grannysbooks.com**–A wonderful resource!!!! It gives information on great books for boys and girls sorted by age, gender, and/or subject.

Tried and True!

In all my years of teaching and few at grandmothering, I have found a number of books that all of the children seem to enjoy.   Listed below are some favorites for various times and events throughout the year. Children don't seem to mind when you read their favorite books; for example, as far as they are concerned, a Christmas book may be read anytime during the year.

VALENTINE'S DAY (Good for teaching about love, friendships and relationships)
 Hearts, Cupids, and Red Roses:
  The Story of Valentine Symbols, Barth
 What is Valentine's Day? Ziefert
 Somebody Loves You, Mr. Hatch , Spinelli
 It's Valentine's Day,
  a book of poems by Jack Prelutsky
  "I Love You More than Applesauce", a favorite!
 Valentine Friends, Schweninger
 The Mysterious Valentine, Carlson
 How Spider Saved Valentine's Day, Kraus
 One Zillion Valentines, Modell
 One Very Best Valentine's Day
 Valentine Kittens, St. Pierre

Dinosaur Valentine, Donnelly

The Valentine Bears, Bunting

The Man Who Kept His Heart in a Bucket, Levitin

Valentine's Day Grump, Greydanus

Arthur's Valentine, Brown

Things to Make and Do on Valentine's Day, Paola

EASTER

Lilies, Rabbits and Painted Eggs:
  The Story of the Easter Symbols, Barth

The Country Bunny and the Little Gold Shoes,
  Heyward

How Spider Saved Easter, Kraus

The Story of Easter for Children, Ideals

Peter Rabbit, Potter

Bunnies Love, McCue

The Magic Easter Egg, Blevins

The Runaway Bunny. Brown

The Great Big Especially Beautiful Easter Egg,
  Stevenson

The Golden Egg Book, Brown

The Bunnies' Alphabet Eggs, Bassett

Stepka and the Magic Fire, Van Woerkom

Wonders of the Seasons, Parker

Spring Is Here, Taro Gomi

Terry's Caterpillar, Selsam

The Very Hungry Caterpillar, Carle

Any children's books about Spring will reinforce the story of Easter.

THANKSGIVING

Turkeys, Pilgrims, and Indian Corn:
    The Story of the Thanksgiving Symbols, Barth
Three Young Pilgrims, Harness
Oh, What a Thanksgiving! Kroll
The Pilgrims of Plimoth, Sewall
Sarah Morton's Day, Waters
Samuel Eaton's Day, Waters
If You Sailed on the Mayflower in 1620,
    McGovern
Squanto and the First Thanksgiving, Kessel
Silly Tilly's Thanksgiving Dinner, Hoban
Plimoth Plantation, Travers
Cranberry Thanksgiving, Devlin

CHRISTMAS

Christmas Story (pop-up), Paola
Baby's First Nativity (Board Book), Singer
The Littlest Angel, Tazewell
The Night Before Christmas, Moore
The Cobweb Christmas, Climo
La Befana (Italian folk tale)
Christmas Around the World, Kelley
Santa's Surprise Book, Elwart
Santa's Toy Shop, Disney
Jingle Bells, Daly
Baby's Christmas, Wilkin
Rudolph, the Red-Nosed Reindeer, Hazen
The Smallest Elf, Ingle
The Very Best Christmas Present, Razzi
Twelve Bells for Santa (I Can Read book), Bonsall

Merry Christmas, Mom and Dad, Mayer
The Shoemaker and the Christmas Elves,
    Lawrence & Hildebrandt
On Christmas Day (A Playtime Pop-Up), Paris
The Best Christmas Pageant Ever, Robinson
Twelve Days of Christmas
    (beautiful pop-up book), Sabuda

Using Stories
to Teach Grandchildren
how to Make Friends

One of the areas of concern with our grandchildren is their ability to make wise choices regarding their friendships. In fact, children worry themselves that they will not be able to make the "right" friends. Perhaps this is an area in which we, as grandmothers, can help them. It is, indeed, vital to their self-esteem. Listed below are some of the books I have used in teaching this important skill in the classroom:

We Are Best Friends, Aliki. Moving away from a best friend is painful, but we can make new friends.

Best Friends, Cohen. A great story about wanting to have a best friend at school.

Corduroy, Freeman. A teddy bear, Corduroy, finds a friend in a department store.

Chester's Way, Henkes. Two mice experience changes in their friendship.

A Bargain for Frances, Hoban. Frances and a friend have a disagreement over a tea set.

Best Friends, Kellogg. A girl is lonely when her best friend goes away for the summer.

Frog and Toad are Friends, Lobel. Five short stories about the adventures of two friends.

Frog and Toad Together, Lobel. Stories about the wonderful friendship of Frog and Toad.

George and Martha, Marshall. A story about two hippopotamuses who are friends.

Ira Sleeps Over, Waber. Ira spends his first night away from home with a friend.

Will I Have a Friend? Cohen. On his first day of school, Jim wonders if he will have a friend.

Little Bear's Friend, Minarik. Four short stories about Little Bear's friends. A favorite!!

That's What a Friend Is, Hallinan. All of the things a friend is–in verse.

Just My Friend and Me, Mayer. Typical fun time for two little boys.

Together, Lyon. A beautifully illustrated book showing the importance of working together.

Amigo, Baylor.   A poignant story of the friendship that develops between a boy and a prairie dog.

I Know a Lady, Zolotov.   Shows how an older person can become a friend and influence.

A Cup of Christmas Tea.   Tells how we can relate to and learn from the elderly.

10 Ways to Spoil your Grandchild

by Vicki Lansky, *Family Circle* magazine,
September 1, 1997, page 118.

$\mathcal{C}$elebrate Grandparents' Day (September 7) every
day with these great ideas!

1. Spoil your grandchild! – with the parents'
   permission, of course. It's a grandparents'
   right–and responsibility–as well as a grandchild's
   expectation. Just make it a point to spoil all of your
   grandchildren equally.

2. Hide a little something (a stick of gum, a quarter,
   a note) before you leave your grandchild's house
   (under the pillow, in the sock drawer, anywhere).
   With your final goodbye or when you next speak to
   your grandchild on the phone, give clues to find the
   surprise.

3. Preserve your grandchild's adorable sayings in a
   quote book you can give him or her years later.
   Parents often forget to record such gems.

4. Create a postcard collection for the grandkids by sending them one from every place you visit, or put them in a photo album. Dream about visiting these places together some day.

5. Plant a tree on the birth of each grandchild. Take a picture of the tree on your grandchild's birthday to send along each year. If your grandchild lives nearby, take a picture of her with the tree each year.

6. Save different-size boxes for your grandkids to build playhouses or forts with when they come to your home. The boxes can be folded and stored without taking up much space.

7. Keep a box of old clothes, handbags, shoes and the like for visiting grandchildren to play "dress-up". Periodically add things to the box so there is always something new in it.

8. When they visit, schedule a "Granny School" session. Each day devote an hour to reading a book or working on a craft project with one or more of your grandchildren.

9. For the young reader, start your own Grand-Book-of-the-Month Club. Send one book (perhaps part of a series) at the start of the month to your grandchild. Then discuss it the next time you talk.

10. To remain a special and well-loved grandparent, remember that advice that is not asked for is advice that should not be given.

Appendix D:

GRANDPARENTS WHO
ARE PARENTS

think this book would not be complete without giving recognition to those grandparents, who have assumed, for whatever reason, the role of "parent". There *are* an increasing number of grandmothers who must "parent" their grandchildren. I would like to share an article from the *Daily Oklahoman*, written by Charlotte Lankard (January 20, 2003). It is a well-deserved tribute to these selfless individuals, and Ms. Lankard identifies sources of help for these brave folks!

Raising Grandkids Not Easy

Holidays brought grandchildren, and I looked forward to that. Now that they've returned home, I find I am exhausted. I only had them for 10 days, most of the time with a parent, aunt, uncle or cousin to help.

I found myself thinking about those grandparents who are raising their grandchildren. I have a new appreciation for them. While it is nothing new, statistics show it is becoming more common.

The Brookdale Grandparent Caregiver Information Project, based at the University of California at Berkeley Center on Aging, has said that in the past 10 years, the number of children living with their grandparents has increased 50 percent.

It is not something that happens to a particular race, area or social class. It happens in all socioeconomic groups, because of divorce, neglect, teenage pregnancy, the death of parents, incarceration, unemployment, abuse, alcohol or drug use, or abandonment. It can happen to any of us.

When grandparents take on a parental role, their stress increases. Their married life is affected, concerns about their own health increase, and finances have to be managed differently. Finding medical care for the children may be difficult.

Grandparents no longer have much time for themselves, and their dream for retirement may change radically. Their friendships may change, because they no longer have as much in common with people their age.

Feelings will run rampant and range from anger, fear, exhaustion, resentment, grief and shame to thankfulness and joy. All of those are normal and not to be judged. We can be judged for how we behave but not for what we feel.

If you find yourself in this role, you are not alone. There is help. One of the best resources is the AARP Grandparent Information Center. Call (800) 424-3410, write to 601 E Street NW, Washington, DC 20049, or visit the web site www.aarp.org/confacts/programs/gic.html.

The AARP center offers where-to-go suggestions for help with legal issues, financial assistance, finding health care/insurance for the grandchildren, finding quality child care, enrolling the grandchild in school, dealing with psychological/emotional problems, support groups and free services, as well as referrals to other useful web sites.

These grandparents also need a break from the children now and then. That's where you and I come in. Take the kids to a movie, the zoo, or a museum. Prepare a casserole or cookies for the freezer or just listen when they need to complain.

Despite the stress, grandparents raising their grandchildren often say they feel a greater sense of purpose and feel younger and more active. Many think the sacrifices are worth it.

My hat is off to them! Please join me in a round of applause.

About the Author

Toni Stone, who was a school teacher for almost 20 years, collaborated with her students in 1984 in writing *Campbell County Chronicles: The Way We Were*, the history of Campbell Country, Wyoming. The popularity of the book resulted in three printings and earned her the Wyoming's "History Teacher of the Year Award". The following year she guided her students in writing two books of poetry, one written and illustrated by her ninth grade class, the other by her 7th grade class in Gillette, Wyoming.

This book, *I'm a Grandmother!! Now What?!* is a perfect gift for Holidays, Birthdays, Mothers' Day, Grandparents' Day, and baby showers – to congratulate the grandmothers.

To order additional copies as gifts for your friends, please contact AuthorHouse at:

AuthorHouse™

1663 Liberty Drive, Suite 200
Bloomington, IN 47403
www.authorhouse.com
Phone: 1-800-839-8640

OR

AuthorHouse™ UK Ltd.

500 Avebury Boulevard
Central Milton Keynes, MK9 2BE
www.authorhouse.co.uk
Phone: 08001974150

Made in the USA
Lexington, KY
25 June 2012